GARY MCDOUGALL

Don't Tell Me There Ain't No God

KENGAR PUBLISHING

Books That Inspire

First published by KenGar Publishing 2019

Library of Congress Cataloging-in-Publication Data

McDougall, Gary

Dont Tell Me There Aint No God / Gary McDougall

pages cm

Cover Design: SelfPubBookCovers.com/JayF

First edition

ISBN: 978-1-64606-188-4

This book was professionally typeset on Reedsy.
Find out more at reedsy.com

This book is dedicated to my wife, Kendra, daughter, Kiana, and my son, Jayden, whom I love more than words can express. It is my fervent prayer that they find their faith as I found mine and know the Lord as I know Him.

Contents

Acknowledgement

The events described in this book are true as I remember them. Some names have been changed to protect privacy. Nothing in this book is meant to besmirch any person or institution. When an entity or institution is mentioned, it is in the context of the event related to an individual, named or unnamed, and not the entity or institution itself.

I would like to thank my heavenly Father and my Lord and Savior Jesus Christ for empowering me to give this testimony I've come to know as my life. I thank my wife and children for supporting me in this effort and allowing me the space to complete the work.

Thanks to StoryTerrace for helping make this book a reality; and special thanks to John Feldman for his contribution to this work.

It is my hope that all who read this book be inspired to achieve their manifest destiny.

Introduction

My name is Gary McDougall. As a child growing up, I thought the American Dream was just a fantasy. But with hard work and a lot of perseverance, I achieved it.

My life has not been an ordinary one. From what you are about to read, you'll certainly find that out. As I've spoken to people over the course of my life, both personally and professionally, I have heard some of the most astonished reactions: *That really happened? You survived* what? *How are you even still* here?

Funny thing is, I've never asked myself these questions. For my entire life, I've always assumed that what was happening to me was normal. The physical abuse and sexual abuse, poverty, racism, despair, emotional trauma—I thought it was all normal. I thought that what I was going through was what everyone else in the world was going through, but through these conversations I was having, I began to find out I was wrong.

I was living a much tougher life than the average person.

I did. I lived a rough life. So rough in fact, that it brought me to the brink of suicide. I had a plan in place and I was ready to execute. In my mind, there just wasn't a reason to be here anymore. Nothing was going right. Nothing in my life was amounting to anything. I felt useless.

That's when I got my sign from God.

The story I'm about to tell you is my way of unraveling everything.

There are things in this book that I've never discussed with another living soul. Things I told myself I'd keep inside me forever. But I'm letting them out now because it's time. God has put me on Earth for a reason and I believe that this book will reveal just that.

I

BEFORE FAITH

1

HURRICANE HATTIE

I was in fourth grade when I had my first dance with the Devil. I was living in Belize[1] at the time with my mother and five of my siblings. We lived in a small neighborhood called Cinderella Town, but the disaster that took place on Halloween night of 1961 made for a story that could never be called a Cinderella story.

By the time I was in fourth grade, I'd been back and forth between *my* birthplace of the United States and *my parents'* birthplace of Belize several times. Since I was born—and several siblings after—we lived in the United States. It wasn't all glamour though. My mother and father had a relationship that was anything but stable, and after some incident (I still have no idea what it was) my mother took us and went back to Belize, leaving my father in Brooklyn, New York. In fact, I still have a telegram that she sent to him in 1959 letting him know that we had arrived back in Belize safely.

I always saw my mother as a remarkable woman, and the more you read of this book, the more you'll be able to see why. The fact that she managed to make a happy life out of a relationship with my father was amazing enough, but she did so much more.

3

Halloween night in 1961 was one of those nights.

In 1961, there was no Weather Channel, especially not in Belize, but somehow my mother had heard about this hurricane out in the Caribbean and knew it was coming through. She knew about it but we didn't leave the house. The skies outside grew darker and she eventually asked me—*me*, a boy sixteen days shy of my eighth birthday—if we should leave. As crazy as it sounds that *she* asked *me*, the crazier part is that I said no. Maybe it was the brave little boy in me that wanted to hunker down and wait out the storm. Who knows? What I do know is that I said no.

The skies grew even darker, the wind picked up, and it began to rain harder, and then my mother asked me again, "Should we leave?" This time, I said yes. We needed to worry about all of us getting out: Mom, Robert, Wayne, Felicia, Patricia (who was just an infant at the time) and me. The weather was getting bad and we all needed to get somewhere safe.

In the small Caribbean countries like Belize, most everyone is Catholic. At the time, I was already baptized and had made my Holy Communion. I was brought up into the Catholic life and this would play a pretty important role down the road. But for now, I was a little Catholic boy with my Catholic family and we needed to get somewhere that would protect us from the storm.

The first place we could think to go was the church. So we did.

Our house in Cinderella Town was tiny. It had two rooms and a kitchen and it stood up on stilts. The house actually still stands to this day. Right across the street from that house was a church, and next to that church was the school. Our house was small and our town was small and everything I remember doing was in that small, little space, but it was what we knew. When we walked out of the front door to look for a safe spot, we walked right across the street and into that church.

What we found when we walked outside was that the weather was worse than what we thought. The winds were so intense by this point that we struggled to get across the street and into the church. It wasn't easy, but we made it.

We were in the place of God now and everyone felt safe. Many people from Cinderella Town were already there, as was the priest, and everyone was praying and singing—hunkering down and hoping for the best. Everyone had a sense of hope, but hope went out the window when the roof was ripped off.

The church wasn't large, but it had this tall bell tower on top. The wind outside became so intense that the bell tower was ripped clean off and when the churchgoers inside looked up and saw the sky, everyone started running. As we all ran out of the church and looked for another safe spot, the priest stayed back. I never did get proof, but I heard that he had his own little safe spot in the form of a second-story loft.

For the rest of us that ran, we all went next door and into the school. The school was made of cinder block and designed almost like a strip mall—all classrooms lined up next to each other, side by side. The cinderblock structure wasn't only on the perimeter of the entire building, but between each classroom, too. For this reason, everyone thought it would be safest.

It wasn't.

I'd later learn that Hurricane Hattie[2] struck Cinderella Town with all its glory. Our little town was right on the eastern coastline of Belize and when the hurricane slammed into us, it brought all its might. After it had its way with the place we loved, it was documented as one of the most powerful hurricanes to hit North America up until that time. The wind speeds were gusting at 200 mph and the ocean waves were 25 feet high. But the worst part—the part that proved most deadly—was the storm surge that came after.

The winds had torn roofs off of part of the school and caused chaos. To remain safe, everyone ran to the end of the row where a partial roof remained. Once there, the wind finally died down. Everything stopped. Heavy rains and wind gusts went off in the distance. Out of nowhere, it was silent—so quiet you could hear a pin drop. There were no animals or birds or insects—all long gone. It was just us, hidden inside the school, and that was when the water started to pour in. The storm surge was coming. I remember everyone screaming, trying to stand on desks and chairs to stay above water.

My mother has amazed me in many ways throughout my life and this was one of the first ones I can remember. As the waters began to rise, she and another woman swam my two brothers, two sisters, and me out of the building and to telephone poles where they tied us to them using sheets or something (I'm not sure). As the waters rose, they would move us higher. This continued until we were at the top of the posts and then when the water began to recede, they swam us over to the roof of our house. Then when the water levels got low enough, my siblings and I were brought into the house through the windows by my mother and the other woman. That was where we stayed until the storm surge was sucked back out into the Caribbean Sea.

It might have been a day, maybe two, until that happened and all that remained were puddles on the streets. Mom said she wanted to leave and when I asked where we could go, she said we were going to try to go into the city. So that's where we headed.

When we left the house and began walking down the streets, we saw nothing but death—dead people, dead animals—death everywhere. There was nobody. It was quiet and we just kept walking. We walked until we were spotted by soldiers driving around. They picked us up and drove us to a hotel called the St. George Hotel where the Red Cross was set up.

Of the people who stayed behind in Cinderella Town during the hurricane, we were the only known survivors. We stayed in that hotel for a few days and then we ended up at the Belize Airport, sleeping there with a bunch of other survivors. Then my mom worked her miracles once more, somehow managing to get us onto a plane to Miami. There were cargo planes that were flying in and out of the Belize Airport to bring supplies for the survivors, and somehow she managed to get us onto a plane that was heading out. We were destined to get away from the disaster, on our way to the United States to stay with some of my mother's relatives. We'd be safe after all.

Not quite.

As we sat in the cargo area of that plane—Mom, my two sisters, my two brothers, and me—thinking we would soon be safely landing in sunny Miami, we were hit with the reality that the plane didn't have enough fuel to make it. We, the extra cargo, had caused the small plane to need more fuel than anticipated, and we lost an engine, which caused us to almost crash in the Atlantic Ocean.

We made it to land. The plane made an emergency landing somewhere near Miami, but it was costly. It took Mom 40 years before she'd step foot on another airplane after that. Me? I wasn't so scared, but that was because I was just a little kid. I didn't realize how close I was to dying that day, or even a few days prior during the hurricane. I'd nearly lost my life twice in that few-days span, but I managed to survive. I would go on to have many more scenarios in my life where I narrowly escaped with my life, but this was just the beginning.

Gary McDougall would live through Hurricane Hattie and the

near-wreck on the way to Miami. I would live to carry on the name McDougall. The name got its roots in Belize and it all started with a shipwreck.

2

THE MCDOUGALL NAME

I 've read many stories before that are similar to this one, and most of them begin with the birth of the author. But with my story, it goes back further than that. My story goes back to my grandfather.

My last name has confused some people over the years, and this will show true with one instance in particular (more on that later). McDougall is a Scottish name and it roots all the way back to my grandfather, a white man who settled in Belize and married a local woman.

My grandfather, Simon, came to the new world from Scotland in the mid-1800s. His ship was wrecked in the Caribbean Sea after he ran into a barrier reef off of Belize's coast. At the time, not many knew about the reefs in the Caribbean, but it turns out the largest coral reef system in the Western Hemisphere, the Mesoamerican Barrier Reef System, lines the coast of Belize. My grandfather was one of many seafarers whose ships fell victim to this system. With his ship wrecked, he made his way to the coastline and found the place he'd call home. While there, he met and married my grandmother, Ianthee, a Kriol and native of Belize.

The Belizean Kriol[3] people are people living in Belize who have African blood. In the eighteenth and nineteenth centuries, African slaves were brought over to Belize, then called British Honduras, by British settlers. Basically, the same thing that happened here in the United States had also happened there, and those were the descendants of my grandmother.

My grandfather married my grandmother and settled on 90 acres of land. It was turned into a town that they called Sittee River, and my extended family still owns this town today. They live on the land just as their ancestors had, no plumbing and very little electricity. They use outhouses for the bathroom and showers, and there's only one phone in the entire village. One single phone. If you call the village to look for someone, one of my cousins might pick up the phone and ask who you want to speak with. Then they'll have to run around the village to try to find that person. It's a bit different than the life we're living here in the United States, don't you think?

I never got the chance to meet my grandfather, though I wish I would have. I don't even have any pictures of him. Prior to Hurricane Hattie in 1961, Belize went through another hurricane in 1931. During that storm, I've been told that all of my grandfather's pictures were washed away. I have some photos of my grandmother but none of him.

While they lived in Sittee River, my grandparents had six sons together and my father was the youngest of those six sons. One day, the local Constable for a wide area of Belize made his way to Sittee River and brought his daughter, Mabel, with him. The Constable's daughter was my mother, and by her father taking her with him to Sittee River, she met the youngest of the McDougall boys, Herman.

My father was considered by some of my relatives to be a hustler

10

and he used those abilities to convince my mother that he could sneak the two of them into America. I'm not sure how long it was between his promise to her and the promise paying off, but when my mom was several months pregnant with me, my parents snuck across the border and into the United States. They came across the border from Tijuana on the west coast of Mexico and landed in San Diego. Once they got there, they were safe.

It was much easier to get into the country back then than it is now. The same can be said for an undocumented immigrant getting work. Although it was easier back then than it is now, it still couldn't have been easy for my dad to find employment, but he did. He ended up getting a job at a shipyard in San Diego.

A few months after being in San Diego, my parents got their wish—they had an *anchor baby.* I was born at Mercy Hospital in San Diego on November 16, 1953, and since I was born on United States soil, I was a United States citizen. My mother went through a life of hell because of my father, but she did everything for her children. Sneaking across the border in order to ensure I'd be a United States citizen was the first of many sacrifices she'd make.

3

SILVER STAR

Six months after I was born we were on the move again. This time we went to Brooklyn, New York. We lived there for five years and I was given a few brothers and sisters during that time.

In 1959, my mother went back to Belize and she took all of the kids with her, minus Jerome. My brother, Jerome, stayed back with my dad for some reason, and I think it had something to do with him possibly being undocumented and my mother not having any paperwork on him. So he stayed and the rest of us left.

At this point, there were four of us, and she might have even been pregnant when we went back. I was still young (five years old, I think) and the only reason I knew we went back in 1959 was because of a telegram I found in my dad's belongings. The telegram was sent to him from my mother letting him know that we had made it back to Belize safely.

My mother was an amazing woman. She put up with a lot with my dad, and we'll see that as we get farther into the story. In 1959, she left him and I never found out the reason, but whatever happened was bad enough that she packed up her life and her kids and went back to Belize.

I think it's been said that your first real memories in life start when you're about four or five years old, and this was the case for me. The first thing I remember about my life was growing up in Belize. I remember seeing my first movie at about this age; I saw *The Ten Commandments*. I also remember that we arrived in Belize right about the time I was starting kindergarten and we stayed through the fourth grade when Hurricane Hattie hit and drove us back into the open arms of the United States.

After my mother was able to create her miracle and save all of us from the storm surge brought on by the hurricane, we had our plane scare and then made it to Miami. Once there, we stayed with some of Mom's relatives who we knew as the Murphys. The Murphys allowed us to stay with them for a few weeks, but then my mother decided that she wanted to go back to New York to be with my father.

After leaving him before, it was surprising that my mother wanted to go back. She had been without him for years and managed to do just fine. Maybe being back in the United States made her think of him. Whatever the reason, it surprises me to this day that she wanted to go back, but what was even more surprising was the way she was able to get us there.

Back then in 1961, there was a famous train that ran from Miami to New York City called the Silver Star[4]. It first began running in 1947, and up until then, there was apparently never a person or family of color that rode the train as a passenger in one of the sleeper cars. According to my mother and the story she told, we were the first. It made the train ride a bit displeasing for us. That, or maybe it was our behavior.

As if my mother hadn't been through enough, we made it harder on her. My siblings and I were just a bunch of kids who were

13

able to get on a train, and we acted accordingly. Being the first family of color in the sleeper car made the other passengers and workers look at us a little more skeptical than they would the other passengers, although at the time I didn't notice. What *I* noticed, and what *my siblings* noticed, was that we were on a train. A new environment. Somewhere exciting and fun and with a ton of hiding spots. We almost got kicked off the train because of it.

We were rowdy on that train ride and my mother had to tell us to settle down. They already didn't like us being on the train to begin with and now we were making it easier for them to kick us off. All of us kids running around and causing chaos was giving them a reason to throw us off. We behaved as best a group of kids stuck on a train for three days *could* behave. We made it to Grand Central Station in New York, and then finally, to my father's place in Brooklyn.

I'm not sure what my mother was hoping for in a reunion with my father but I'm sure it didn't turn out the way she anticipated. The next few years with my father would lead to some bad experiences, and I'd eventually have to become a man much earlier than I should have.

14

4

I MEANT BUSINESS

When I was nine years old, I started my own shoe-shining business and I did pretty well for myself. I charged a quarter per shine, but I would also get tips sometimes because I made the guys laugh. I played this little music to go along with the way I'd swipe my rag across their shoes—*pop pop pop-pop, pop-pop pop POP!* Some of the guys wouldn't even want their shoes shined. They'd just sit down in the chair and tell me, "Do that pop thing!" Then they'd pay me for it.

I made about ten or twelve dollars a week doing this, which wasn't bad for a nine-year-old, especially in the 1960s. I was a good businessman, though. I took my money at the end of every week and went down and bought me some more shoe-shining supplies. I knew I'd need more if I wanted to keep shining shoes, and with the money left over, I bought myself some glazed doughnuts. Those glazed doughnuts were so good, and they made all the hard work worth it.

I never bought clothes with the money. I wouldn't buy my own new clothes until I was sixteen years old and got a job making 42 dollars per week. The first check I got while working, I went out and bought some shoes. Up until then, we got our clothes from the Salvation Army. We didn't have much luck with shoes either. Ironically, the little boy who shined nice shoes didn't have a pair of his own. Not a nice pair, anyway. I had a pair of sneakers and a pair of shoes for church—my mother said sneakers weren't acceptable for mass.

I wore my church shoes to church and my sneakers everywhere else, but they were so old and worn that I used to cut up pieces of cardboard and put them into the soles once the actual ones wore out. If the cardboard got wet, though, they'd be ruined. So I'd always have spare pieces of cardboard cut up and ready to go if I needed them.

When we moved into my father's apartment in Brooklyn, things were tight. He lived in a small, two-bedroom place on the second floor above a bar. There were seven of us kids living there at the time and we all shared a room. We'd sleep on these little twin beds that folded out. At night, we'd sleep with one eye open because there were rats running around and we'd be afraid to get bitten by them. Also at night, we'd hear the music, drunkenness, fights, and all the other commotion that went on down at the bar. But the people that made all the noise down there ended up being my customers. When I bought my first shoe-shining kit, I went downstairs in front of that bar and caught the guys as they'd go in and out. It didn't take them long to get to know who I was and to start coming back as repeat customers.

In the wintertime, though, I closed up shop. We were from Belize where cold winters aren't a thing. In Belize, every day is hot. Brooklyn was a big change of pace. It was in Brooklyn that we got to see our first snowfall. It was an amazing experience, but also scary. That first snowstorm we were a part of in Brooklyn was a major one. There was so much snow that it came up against the door to our place and we couldn't even open it. The scariest part was we were out playing on the fire escape and Jerome somehow fell off. We looked over and we all started freaking out. He'd fallen from the second story and down into the snow and all you could see was the hole where he fell. That's how deep the snow was. He wasn't big enough to get up and out of the snow on his own and we all thought he was going to drown. Remember, this was our first experience with snow and we didn't even really know how it worked, so we all started screaming.

Luckily, our screaming worked. It got the attention of someone—a man, I don't even know who it was—but that man went and got Jerome out of the snow, brought him back to the door that wouldn't open, somehow managed to open it, and then got Jerome back inside safely.

I had some scares when we were living here, too. This will become something of a recurring theme. By this time in my life, I was ten years old and I'd already lived through Hurricane Hattie and the flight back to Miami that almost crashed into the Atlantic Ocean. Both of these moments were moments that most people don't live *one* of, but I lived both in the span of a few days. That wouldn't be it for me, though. These dances with death, or near-death experiences, cheating death events or whatever you want to call them. They came often for me.

The next one came right around the same time I was doing my shoe-shining thing. I was asleep one night and got up and walked in to sleep next to my mom. Since the apartment was so small, I was practically in the same room even though I went to sleep beside her instead of in my own bed. But if I hadn't made that short walk over to her, *cheating death* might not have been the story being told, and there'd be no more text to write after this paragraph.

I had peanuts earlier in the day, according to my mother, and while sleeping in the middle of the night, I started choking. She woke up at the sound of my gasping for air and then realized that choking had turned into not breathing. Back then, there was no 911 to call when you have emergencies like this, but there *was* a fire department, and my mom was smart enough to call them in the midst of the chaos. They came, turned me upside down, and shook me like a bully looking for change. No change came out of my pockets, but those peanuts did come out of my throat.

Not long after that, I had another freak accident happen. This one won't really qualify as a near-death experience, but it was certainly nearly life-altering. In our little apartment, there was a closet in the room where my parents slept and that closet had a hole in the top of it. Being a kid, I would spy on my dad, and one time it didn't turn out so well. One time, I wasn't as stealthy as I thought and he caught me. I jumped, stumbled, and fell back. During the fall, my eye got caught on a nail that was hanging out of the wall. The nail ripped my eyelid clean off. Gone. It fell onto the ground and I have no idea what type of sound it made when it hit. I was too busy screaming and looking at the blood.

Once again, there was no 911, so my mom picked up my eyelid and wrapped it up into a piece of tissue. Then we got onto the bus and went to the hospital. The doctors saw me and told my mother it was a good thing she kept my eyelid the way it was. Because of her, they were able to sew it back on, and to this day, that eyelid works perfectly fine.

The process of getting it put back on was also pretty memorable because anesthesia was involved. During the procedure, the surgeons needed to put me under with anesthesia so I wouldn't blink or anything while they were trying to put it back. When I came to, groggy from the medicine, all I heard were people crying. I thought I was dead. I thought to myself that everyone was crying because I'd died. That could be the only reason. I died and they were all so sad to have lost me. It wasn't the reason for the crying, of course. The reason everyone was crying was because the date was November 22, 1963, the day JFK was shot. When I awoke in the recovery room of the hospital, the news was just breaking out about Kennedy's assassination. People always ask if you remember where you were on major occasions and I will always remember exactly where I was when John F. Kennedy was assassinated.

The tiny apartment with holes above closets, nails hanging out, and rats running around was luckily only a temporary place of residence for us. In 1963, a new area of government housing projects was being built in Staten Island, New York[5]. My dad applied to get in and we did. We had a brand-new home on the fourth floor of a brand-new housing project. It had four bedrooms, more than one bathroom, and was giant compared to the apartment in Brooklyn.

I was ten or eleven years old when we moved into the Staten Island projects, and I'm not sure if it was because I was older or that I just never realized it before, but I started to see how abusive my dad was. He wasn't just exclusively abusive to my mother, either. He beat us, too. He was an equal opportunity beater.

One night my sister, Felicia, and I snuck out of the house, and when we came home, he was on the couch. He knew we were out and he stayed up to wait for us. He and I started getting into it a little bit and it got physical. He grabbed me and dragged me out to the window of our new fourth-floor home and then held me out the window by my ankle like he was going to drop me. My mom and sister were screaming at him, "Don't drop him! Please don't kill him!" He didn't. He dragged me back in through the window and dropped me on the floor.

19

Living with my father was tough. He was a drinker, which might have been his problem. He'd stop at the bar on his way home from work every day and then he'd come home miserable. He was a miserable person to begin with, but I think the alcohol made it worse. My father was such a bad person that, one day, he bought a steak from the store, brought it home, and made my mom cook it for him. Then he ate the entire thing right in front of us all. He didn't offer any of us anything. We had to have the rice and beans, or whatever else we were going to have that our mother made, but he had his steak and ate the whole thing right in front of us.

Come to think of it, he must have *ordered* my mother to cook his steak rather than ask her. He spoke to her without an ounce of respect. I never even heard him call her by her first name. His name for her was "Woman." When he'd want something, he'd yell at her, "Woman!" A great role model for a young boy.

My dad abused us a lot and I remember the night it got really bad. I was twelve years old at the time. I heard a bunch of noise in the kitchen and came out to see my mother in the middle of the kitchen floor with dishes smashed all around her. Her face was all bruised from being hit and she took it out on the dishes because taking it out on my dad wasn't a choice. I remember seeing her like that and my face grew hot with rage. I was so over his antics.

This had been going on for too long. He had beaten my mom, and beaten us, and I was over it. So while my mom sat on the kitchen floor crying, I ran into my room and got my wooden baseball bat. I ran out into the living room with the bat in my hand and stopped where he sat on the couch. I said to him, "If you ever touch my mother again, or anyone else in this house, I will wait until you fall asleep and then I will bash your head in and kill you."

And I would have.

5

CURSE THE SKY

As badly as I'm sure he wanted to, my dad couldn't beat me after I threatened him with my little league bat. I mean, he could have, but he knew it would be the last time. He could tell I was serious about what I said, and if he beat me, he'd never be able to sleep again. I was ready to follow through with that threat. It had to stop somewhere.

The police ended up being called anyway. The fight was loud, and surely after my mother started smashing dishes all over the kitchen, it got louder. Some of the neighbors ended up calling the police and they came and arrested my dad. They *had* to. As soon as they showed up at the door and saw my mother's swollen and bloody face they were left with no choice.

The police ended up letting him go, though, because my mother wouldn't press charges against him. If she pressed charges against him, the police would have found out that neither of them were in the country legally, and they both would have been deported and she didn't want that to happen.

When she didn't press charges, the police released him and he came back to the apartment, but things were never the same. When he came back, he didn't lay a hand on any of us again, but he didn't stay long enough to be tempted to. After only a few more weeks living with us, he took off, got his own apartment in Brooklyn, and left us in Staten Island.

When he left us, he left us with nothing. We went from being sort of broke to being *completely* broke because my mother wasn't working. Had she known he was going to leave, she might have tried to get a job, but she didn't know. None of us did.

As she always did, my mother did what she had to do for her children. We went and signed up for welfare and food stamps. I'd go down to the social services depot with her sometimes and we'd have this shopping cart with us where we'd get the food we were given: government cheese, powdered eggs, powdered milk, some beans and rice, and that dreaded Spam. Spam was the one meat that we were allowed to have and we ate it so much that I could never even look at it again once I got older. Still can't. I refuse to eat it.

We made the best of it, though, especially the kids. When we used to run out of food, we would roll up slices of bread like cigars and we'd call them "bread sandwiches." We also got Kool-Aid, but it wasn't the add sugar kind, it was pre-sweetened Kool-Aid. Still tasted good, especially to us kids.

Things continued this way for a few years, right up until about the time I was in high school. By that time, my mother got a job at Willowbrook State School and we were able to get off welfare. She was bringing in money but not a ton of it. By the time she got her job, there were eight kids in total. I'm not sure *any* job she would have gotten could have provided her with enough earnings to raise eight kids on her own.

Finances weren't the greatest, but then again, they weren't great when my father was around either. Regardless, we managed to survive. Surviving elementary school was another story. I was in fifth grade and I was going to public school; PS 31 was its name. However, I was running into issues with bullying and some other stuff going on, so my mother pulled me out of there. She took me out of the public school system and said she was going to send me to Catholic school. Going into Catholic school wasn't anything overwhelming to me. It was what I was used to in Belize. What I *wasn't* used to was being the only black kid enrolled, and when my mother pulled me out of PS 31 and sent me to Saint Peters Elementary, that's what I became. Not only was I the *only* black kid in school, but I was the first to *ever* go there.

My mom pulled me out of PS 31 because I was getting bullied, but when I got to my new school it turned out to be worse. I remember saying to her that at least at PS 31 it was just little pokes and jabs. But at Saint Peters? Those kids called me every racial slur under the sun. I would sit in the corner by myself at recess to avoid it. Sometimes, I wished I was back at public school where the bullying was physical and not emotional.

While this was going on at Saint Peters, the nuns who taught the classes noticed, but they never said anything about it. They didn't care. The only person in the whole school who cared about what was going on was the janitor. He was a black man and he would come up to me and tell me to let it go. To hang in there. Not to let the other kids gets the best of me. But that was easier said than done.

For three years I went to that school, from fifth grade until eighth grade, and I somehow made it into the school's choir program. It was nice but I realized later that the reason for me making it into the program was for political reasons. This was all happening during the civil rights movement, and the school wanted to show everyone, "Look! We have a black kid at our school! We're inclusive!" So they encouraged me to be part of clubs and activities. Our school's choir would sing at church every Sunday and all the participants at Mass could see me—it wasn't hard to miss my face in a sea of white.

Joining the school's choir and singing at Mass every Sunday led me into the one moment that would make me curse the Lord's name. It would be the beginning of a dark time between God and me that would last for a long time.

There was an Irish priest at the church where our choir sang. He wasn't the main priest, but he still participated in the services every Sunday. After mass, he and the others would come up and speak with the members of the choir. One day, this priest came up to me and asked me to meet him at the rectory the next day. I was twelve, and naïve, and did as I was told.

The next day, I showed up to the rectory and asked for Father X (I'm sure he's long gone and dead by now, but I can't remember his name). I walked into the rectory and asked for him, then was given a set of directions to his room. "Go upstairs and he's in that first door right there." *Okay.* I followed the route to his room, and when I got to the door, he was there. Waiting for me, maybe. Or simply there like he was on a normal Monday. He brought me into his room and shut the door. We started talking and then other things started happening. That's about as far as I'll go with the details, and it's probably about as far as you'll want to read a story about a twelve-year-old boy and a priest.

When I left his room that day, I was confused. What the hell just happened? I had never had any sexual experience before and I really didn't even know what it was. There was no Internet back then for curious kids and sexuality wasn't all over television back then like it is today. I had no idea what had just happened and I blamed my dad.

My dad never gave me anything. He never got me gifts or

toys and he never even had the decency to sit with me like a father should and give advice. I never knew about sexuality and pedophiles, and I never even imagined that people did to kids what that priest did to me. All my dad ever did for me was beat me up and yell at me.

This incident happened towards the end of my time at Saint Peter's, at the end of seventh grade, I believe. I continued to go to that school and went on about my life after that day. Then came the end of my reign at the school and the teachers and administrators offered—and pushed me—to go to their high school and continue on with them. They were so nice to me and offered me the opportunity with big smiles, but I told them no. Told them I was done with them. And I remember walking home on that very last day as a student there. I looked up at the sky and I swore the Lord's name. I shook my fist in the air and cursed Him.

How could you let this happen? I hate you!

How could He? How could this God who is responsible for my well-being let this happen? How could He let one of his own priests do this? I'd been a Catholic since birth. I was Baptized, I made my Holy Communion and my Confirmation. I went to church every Sunday and gave money, went to Catholic school, and joined the choir. I did everything the Lord ever asked of me and yet He allowed this to happen to me?

No. I was done with Him. That day, after shaking my fist in the air, I was done. I cut God out of my life after that very moment. I cut out all religion. No more.

6

KILL VAN KULL

New York summers were hot. They were hot and muggy. As a kid growing up in Belize, you wouldn't think I'd find the summers in the northeast to be so bad, but they were. So we'd spend these hot days at Thompkins Pool in Staten Island, which was a public pool. It would cost fifteen cents to get in and then you could swim all day. You could swim right up until they closed and kicked you out.

When school let out, all the kids in the area would hang out at Thompkins Pool. One of those kids was a childhood friend of mine named Billy. He was a skinny little kid, but man was he a good swimmer. He was the same age as I was, twelve at the time, and he could swim well and dive off the high-dive. Basically, he could do a lot of cool things I couldn't and he became my friend that summer because he would teach me all the things he knew.

Billy and I would hang together outside the pool, too. But he was a swimmer. He loved to swim, and during those hot summers, so did I. One of the places we'd go hang out was an old, abandoned factory along the Kill Van Kull[6], which is a waterway that branches off of the Hudson River. The building had this overhang that led out to the waterway, so we'd jump off it and into the water, then climb back up the rocks and into the building, and we'd jump again. It was fun—a little different than the pool—and we didn't have to pay the fifteen cents to do it.

One day, Billy came up with an idea that any two twelve-year-olds would think is great, "Hey, let's swim across to New Jersey!"

The Kill Van Kull is about 1,000 feet wide when measured from one side to the other. On our side, where we jumped from the old building, we were in New York. The land on the other side of the waterway was New Jersey. So for two kids, swimming to another state sounded like an awesome idea. I agreed.

Although the waterway is only 1,000 feet across, it's still a body of water that connects to the Hudson River. Charter and tug boats still run through it and there are still currents and tides and other attributes that bodies of water have. For Billy and me, though, it was just a body of water that we could swim across, go to school in September, and tell stories of how we swam to New Jersey when other kids asked the question, "So what'd you do this summer?"

The plan was to get across and then come back. One thousand feet each way—not too bad. We took off and swam to the other side easily, then climbed up on this pier and rested for a while. Now it was time to go back to the New York side and we both started swimming. This was when the difference between Billy's swimming abilities and mine really showed.

Billy was able to get across quickly, but I got tired. I started switching up my method, doing the backstroke and floating until I regained some energy. But right as I was switching up my style, getting tired, two tugboats started coming down towards me, one from each side. I doubt either of them even saw me—certainly they weren't expecting to see people swimming in the Kill Van Kull—and they kept going on their path. As both passed me on either side, this sort of current formed and it pulled me down the waterway, out towards the Hudson.

This current continued to pull me for about a mile or a mile and a half, and I tried to swim out of it, but I couldn't. As I was going, I saw this buoy coming up and my plan was to grab onto it so I could stop, but as I got closer, I realized how fast I was going—too fast. Now I was headed straight for this thing at a speed way too high to be safe. All I wanted to do at first was to grab it, but now I needed to avoid it. I tried to swim, tried to kick, and finally got out of the way. As the buoy went flying by me, I realized just how lucky I was not to have hit it. Had I hit it, I would have been knocked unconscious and drowned for sure, but being able to escape it had saved me.

What also saved me was *this* thought: swim at an angle. For the mile and a half I'd been dragged down the waterway, I was trying to swim toward the shore only to be pulled back into the belly of this current. If I would have kept trying this method, I would have been pulled all the way out into the New York Harbor.

Swim at an angle. I listened to this thought and I swam at an angle toward the edge, rather than trying to make it in a straight shot, and just before I was sucked out and into the harbor, I reached land. I survived. Then I walked back to the old, abandoned factory to look for Billy to see if he was still looking for me. He wasn't.

I went to Billy's house right after that and he was home. "What the heck?" I asked him. "Why didn't you call somebody?" He ran home after he saw that I was getting carried away. I was so angry at that moment when I saw him, but he said he was sorry and that he was scared. And he was. He was just a little boy. We both were. I wasn't angry at him after that and didn't hold any grudge. We actually remained friends right up until I moved away from the area.

This had been my fifth or sixth near-death experience in my short twelve years on this Earth. At the time, I had no idea just how often I was staring death right in the face. My assumption was that these things happened to everyone and that I was simply living a normal life. It wouldn't be until later that I'd realized just how many times I had experiences like these, and compared to the next time it would happen, this Kill Van Kull story didn't seem so bad because the next near-death experience I would have involved a knife sliding across my neck.

7

HIGH SCHOOL

I happily declined the offer to go to Saint Peters High School after what happened to me with their priest. I instead chose to go to a vocational high school where I could learn a trade that would help me pursue a career. God was no longer a part of my life, nor was religion, and I felt no different.

I'm not sure vocational high schools even exist anymore. These were optional schools that you could attend in place of academic schools. Instead of learning things like math and science, you learned skills that would prepare you for the job market—plumbing, electrical, carpentry, auto mechanics, and other blue-collar careers. The vocational school I went to, McKee High School, had a plan for every incoming freshman: dabble a bit into everything your first year in order to find what you like.

During my freshman year, I found the skill I liked most: auto mechanics. So from my sophomore year on, this was my focus, and I learned a lot. I really did. I was happy with my choice to go to a vocational school over a traditional academic school. Wouldn't have had it any other way. In fact, I learned so much while in my sophomore year that by junior year, I had a full-time job as a mechanic. I was going to school to learn the trade and getting more hands-on experience at night while, most importantly, making money.

By the time I was seventeen, I had seven brothers and sisters. Mom was working at the Willowbrook State School and bringing home *some* money, but she needed help. As the oldest of the eight total kids, I had to be the one to provide the additional income. So I started working and making some decent money.

I started seeing a girl around this time. I think I was seventeen because I was driving her around, but I might have been younger—it's probably safe to say it now, but I was driving illegally before I got my license. I needed to get around in order to make money and I did what I had to do. The money is also the reason I think the girl started seeing me. I was never really one to be smooth with the ladies and I actually had a bit of trouble talking to them. I was never the guy to approach a woman and initiate conversation. Typically, my role was to hang back and hope for the best. With my new job and decent money, sitting back seemed to work for me. At least it did in this instance, anyway.

She was a Puerto Rican girl and we hadn't seen each other much. This might have actually been one of the first times we hung out, but she asked if I could take her home one night, and I did. She lived in Brooklyn which wasn't too far of a drive.

She lived with her mom and when we got to her house, I was invited in. Her mom was there and the three of us were just hanging out, watching TV or something. I can't really remember what. What I *do* remember is this girl leaning over to me after a bit and asking me if she could borrow some money. *Of course you can.*

Not being very good with women, I was easily manipulated. My thought was that everyone was kind-hearted like I was. My father decided to leave before I was twelve, which is prime time for starting to have talks with your son and walk him through life, but without a father, I had to learn everything on my own, mostly through mistakes—*live and learn.*

The girl said she needed the money for her mom (she had to go pick up medicine for her or something). She swore she'd pay it back, but I wasn't too worried about it. Just being in the presence of a pretty girl was fine enough for me, and it wasn't like she was asking to borrow a couple hundred dollars. It was only a few bucks. Nothing much.

I gave her the money and she told me she'd be right back. No problem. I sat there with her mom while she ran to wherever she needed to run to in order to do whatever needed to be done. Time went by slowly and her mom and I just sat on the couch, in silence. She didn't speak any English and you could hear the creak of the chair with every movement. Every breath taken seemed so loud between the two of us. Minutes passed like hours and soon it became apparent that this girl didn't run down the hall to make a phone call. Nor did she quickly walk to the corner store to pick up some medication or groceries her mom needed. Two torturous hours later, I finally caved and went looking for her. Not only did this girl make me drive her home, but she asked to borrow money and then took off. I wanted to know where she was.

Well, I found her, and she wasn't picking up something for her mom. With the money she asked me so sweetly to borrow, she was (I think) buying drugs, and I put "I think" in parentheses because I'm not really sure if she was buying drugs or not. What I *do* know is that when I found her, she was standing on the street with a drug dealer, and when I asked her to come back with me, back to her mom's place, or my car, or anywhere but the dark street, the drug dealer she was with told me, "No, she's not going anywhere with you." Then *she* started to join him, yelling at me and cursing and telling me she wasn't going anywhere with me.

The scene escalated quickly and led to yet another moment where I would stare death directly in its cold, emotionless face. The drug dealer pulled a gun from somewhere—his jacket, waistline—I don't even know. He pointed it right at my face, and without any hesitation, he pulled the trigger.

Click.

My life flashed before my eyes. It's one of the most common expressions you hear people say when they talk about near-death experiences, dances with the Devil, incidences of escaping death, whichever phrase best suits you. And I've had those flashbacks before. They're real and I'll get to those later in the story, but with this particular instance, I had no time. My mind didn't have those moments to process death and the possibility of it. When the drug dealer lifted the gun to my face, he pulled the trigger. No hesitation.

But it misfired, and then I turned and ran like hell. I didn't care about the girl, or the guy, or the mom in the house. I cared about getting as far away from there as possible, and that's exactly what I did. I ran, got to my car, drove home, and didn't look back once. After the drive home, I parked in the lot outside of the projects and sat there for a second, realizing what had just happened. It sent my mind into overload. My body froze. I felt nothing, and it would be like that for two days.

The next morning, my family members began to realize as they woke up that I wasn't home. They all became worried and thought I was missing. Then one of them – I think it was my sister Felicia – had the idea to go look outside to see if my car was there. It was, and so was I, sitting in the same position. They called an ambulance and I was taken to the hospital and declared to have gone into catatonic shock. For two days, I felt nothing. I felt no pain, I didn't move, didn't speak. And then out of nowhere, I just snapped out of it. I was fine.

I never saw that girl again, thankfully, and went on about my life. I was still a kid so I had to go back to school, and I still had a mother to help financially and seven siblings looking to the two of us to provide them with food, shelter, and their other needs. I made it through my senior year of school and expected to graduate, but then something happened. For a couple of students, there was an issue with us graduating—some missed art class or something. It was small, and not anything to do with our occupation, but it was a class that needed to be taken. So in order to graduate and get a diploma, we'd all have to come back the next year and take that course.

My response, "Aww, heck naw." My little catch phrase.

I had a family to help support. I needed to work. My final two years of high school already consisted of going to school full-time and working full-time. I couldn't do it again. Couldn't do another year of going to school, walking down the street to work once school was out, working a full shift, going home, and then sitting down to do my homework. It was exhausting and I was done with it.

The guidance counselor at the vocational school, Mr. Frank Besignano, was a really nice and understanding guy, and he helped me even after I told him I wasn't coming back. "Wait eighteen months," he told me. "Then you can get your GED."

It was a perfect plan and it was what I was going to do. So I left school and I got a job as an auto mechanic at a local K-Mart. It was a good job that paid well and I was really excited to get started, but then some blast from the past came back to haunt me.

When I was fifteen years old, I went to K-Mart with a couple of friends, and the first thing I'll do here is throw up my hands and say that I did *not* participate in what happened. But what *did* happen is that the friends I was with decided to steal from the store. It's been so long that I can't even remember what exactly it was that they took, but whatever it was, they made it out of the store with it all. We all walked out and apparently didn't go far enough before they all started to pull out the things that they took from their jackets or pants or wherever. Once again, I didn't participate and I had nothing to brag about. As a matter of fact, I was in shock when I saw that they all did what they did. Before I could have any sort of reaction to it, though, I was interrupted.

A bunch of fifteen-year-old kids think they're invincible. We were no different. So when my friends walked out the front door of the store, they thought they were free. Now remember, this was at a time when those anti-theft sensors at every exit didn't exist. If you walked out of the store with something, you "made it." The only way to get caught was if someone saw you.

Well, the manager of the store saw everything. He followed us and when the other guys were showing off their loot, the manager of the store approached us, called the cops, and had us all arrested. Ironically enough, three years later I would get a job as an auto mechanic at K-Mart (a different location, of course). Three years after the shoplifting incident where I was arrested, went to court, and put on probation, I was working at the auto shop department of the same franchise, different location. (Back then, K-Mart had an auto department the way Pep Boys has it now.) It was a good job, but low and behold, one day that manager that had me arrested showed up to the shop, saw me, and recognized me. He was coming in to get his car worked on and noticed me right away, years later. Then he went and told the manager of the location where I was working and told them everything.

They fired me on the spot. I never even stole anything and had to go through all of that. Even as a fifteen-year-old, I had to go through the process of getting arrested, going to court, and having to go on probation, and I never took a thing. The job at K-Mart was short-lived, and with nothing lined up, I did what I would eventually do many, many times: I went back to work for the cab company.

8

FALSE PROMISES

I think the cab company I worked for might have been a mafia front. I didn't know it at first. To me, this first job of mine was a great gig. It was just a few blocks away from my high school, I could put in a lot of hours after classes, and I was making good money. But slowly, things began to come into play that would make me think it was a mafia front. The cars pulling into the garage with a trunk full of stolen goods was one indicator, but as I started working there more, the "made" guys would come up and start talking to me. While they never gave away any details, you could just sort of tell who they were.

The garage at the taxi company had some lifts and some pits (lifts are giant jacks that lift a car up so you can get under it and pits are hollowed-out areas beneath the surface that allow you to walk down below and work on a car that way). For the most part, I was working in the pits, and when I would be under there changing oil or anything, I would get covered in the gook and gunk that came out of these engines. Every time I saw or spoke with some of these "made" guys, I would be filthy, oil and fluid all over my face and head. For that reason, they would call me Scuzz. That was my name to them and I didn't really mind. Truth be told, I'm glad I never objected to it. Otherwise, I might have had a second bad experience with the Kill Van Kull and might not have been so lucky this time. The wise guys in this time period were known for tying cinder blocks to their enemies' feet and dumping them into the bodies of water that surrounded New York.

The taxi company was a good job for me but going home and cleaning up after each shift was not. The mafia guys were calling me Scuzz for a reason, because I was always so filthy. I'd go home at night and it would take me ten minutes to scrub the grease from beneath my fingernails. It started to get to me and I wondered if being an auto mechanic was really what I wanted to do with my life.

So I decided to leave the taxi company and get a job working where my mother worked, at the Willowbrook State School[7]. It no longer exists now, but at the time, it was a major focus in the United States. It was a state-run school where kids with extreme mental and physical handicaps would go to be cared for. I worked there as a mental health worker, but more importantly, this was where I met a girl named Eva.

Eva was a supervisor at the school, and when the two of us met, we started hanging out. She didn't have a car so I would drive her home from work. It wasn't a quick trip around the corner. Eva lived in the Lower Eastside of Manhattan, which was a good hour to hour and thirty minutes away. To get to her, I would have to cross over the Verrazano Bridge and the Brooklyn Bridge. The rides weren't pleasant, but we were in love at the time, and I didn't mind doing it for her. It was also some extra time I was able to spend with her.

While I was working at Willowbrook, there was a young, up-and-coming reporter named Geraldo Rivera. You may have heard of him now. Today, he's basically a household name, but back then, he was just a young reporter looking for his big break, and he found it at Willowbrook State School when he came bursting in with cameras rolling after some things were said to be going on there. While the situation wasn't the best, I did see Geraldo Rivera up close and personal when it happened. He was overbearing and coming up to each employee to ask questions. I had no idea what to say when he came into the room I was in. I just looked at him in shock at the chaos he was causing.

Prior to Geraldo storming through the doors with his cameras, Eva and I worked there together. We did a little more than just work together—we fell in love. This was my first experience with loving a woman and I wanted to do a lot for her. One of the things I did was to take her to the Copacabana. It was the super hot club in New York at the time, and not only that, my most favorite band of all time was going to be playing there: The Temptations. I had to save up $100, which was a *whole lot* of money to me at the time, but hey, I was in love and she was worth it.

The Copacabana was a supper club so you weren't sitting up in some balcony seats when you were there. We sat at a table right in the front. The microphones were set up on stands so close we could almost reach out and touch them. The band came out and performed and I'd never felt so important in my life up until then. The date was well worth the money I spent.

A funny story would occur years later from this night. In 1998, a movie came out about The Temptations. Now as a fan, I knew Eddie Kendricks and The Temptations had broken up shortly after that concert, but what I didn't know was that the last time they ever played together was in the Copacabana *that very night*. The movie that came out almost 30 years after their split showed a fight occur between the band where Eddie left, and that fight took place backstage at the Copacabana. All these years, I never knew how close I was to actually witnessing the falling out of one of my favorite bands, and the movie explained to me that I was under the same roof when it happened. Crazy.

Eva and I kept dating, and while it started off nicely, it didn't end so well. One day, she came to me and told me she was pregnant. As an eighteen-year-old, my first instinct was that I wasn't ready for it. I didn't have much money or anything of my own. I had nothing to offer a child and I wasn't ready to take on the responsibility of having one. Eva told me that it was my choice on whether or not we should keep it and I told her exactly what I thought was best for our situation. Like I said, I wasn't ready to bring a child into this world. What could I do for it? Would the kid have to struggle through life the way I did as a child? I didn't want that for any offspring of mine. It wouldn't be fair to them. I wanted to make sure I was financially secure, emotionally secure, and ready to have a kid before actually having one.

Another thought on my mind was my father. It was more of a fear than a thought, as I feared that I would turn out to be exactly like him. I didn't want that. In fact, I told myself many times when I was younger that I *never* wanted to get married or have kids for this exact reason. I didn't want to risk becoming like him.

I told Eva I wasn't ready and that we should abort the child.

There are two parts to my life, "Before Faith" and "After Faith." Before the hand of God came down and rested upon my shoulder, I didn't believe in religion. What the priest did to me when I was twelve years old made me immune to any feelings based on faith, and when this incident occurred, I wasn't thinking the way I would have if I was older and had found my path.

But as an eighteen-year-old, I made the decision I thought was right. While Eva had told me that she would leave the final decision up to me, I feel like she really wanted me to say that

41

we should keep the baby, that I loved her, and that we could have this baby and maybe even start a family together. And when I didn't, it broke her.

After telling her my choice to have an abortion, she said okay, and then I scrounged up the money to have it done. However, when she went to the clinic, the nurse there convinced her that she could have an injection instead of going the traditional route. This way would be less invasive and would simply terminate the pregnancy. After hearing her options, this was the path Eva chose.

It worked. The pregnancy was terminated. A short time after getting the injection though, something happened to Eva that she wasn't expecting—the fetus came out of her one day while she was sitting on the toilet. It freaked her out. She was beside herself, a basket case. She called me, distraught, and through sobs she was able to tell me parts of what happened. I drove over to her mother's house where she lived because her mother wasn't home to help her. When I arrived, she described to me exactly what happened, and I completely understood why she was beside herself. As a man, I have no idea what that feeling could possibly be like. I could never be pregnant and could never have that happen, but I certainly empathized with her.

All the empathy and kindness in the world couldn't take back what happened to her, though. She blamed me for the whole thing, basically telling me that the reason she had the abortion in the first place was because of me. She was ready to have the baby, but I said no so she went through with it.

That day when I left her mother's house was the last time I ever saw Eva. I went back a few days later to try to talk to her and the nurse from the abortion clinic was the one who answered the buzzer to the apartment. "She don't want to talk to you," she told me through the intercom. She must not have, because she never spoke to me again. Not only did Eva leave me, but I found out later that she left me for another woman. She started dating that nurse who answered the intercom shortly after, the one from the abortion clinic who administered the injection, and that was the last I heard of her.

The story was a sad one and as a man of faith now, abortion isn't something I would ever consider. That's not saying I'm here to judge anyone for their actions, nor do I want anyone to judge me for mine, but my thoughts on the subject are much different now. Regardless, I made my decision. I needed to ensure I was financially stable before I had kids and that's what I was going to do.

My guidance counselor from McKee High School told me that eighteen months after choosing not to come back to school, I could go take the test for my GED, and that's exactly what I did. I took the test and passed it with such a high score that I was offered a chance to go to college for free under a program called Advancement on Individual Merit, or AIM. I enrolled in the State University of New York (SUNY) at Stony Brook and chose Urban Planning as my major (going Undecided wasn't an option with AIM).

But I was doing it. I was going to college. I thought about what career I was going to have and how great my life was going to be—going from greasy fingernails to college graduate. Unfortunately, AIM didn't turn out to be as great of a program as it was said to be. I mean, it could have been, if the money granted to the program wasn't embezzled. When I went to register for my second semester of classes, I was told by the SUNY admissions office that my money never cleared for the first semester. I couldn't register for any second semester classes until first semester classes were paid for. I was able to make a few phone calls and resolve the matter, but when it happened again going into my third semester, SUNY simply shook their head at me. *Nope.* I was sent packing. No college degree and no chance of getting one.

What I did gain while at school was an introduction to music. While attending SUNY, I started being a DJ at clubs and parties, and I also got my own little radio show at the school. Back then, disco music was everywhere, and I was one of the ones that brought the music places, brought them to life. I loved it but once I got the boot from the State University of New York, being a DJ got the boot, too. I hung around the area for a little while, crashing on peoples' couches and borrowing meal plan tickets to eat, but that only lasted so long.

On the day I drove home from the SUNY campus, I was miserable. I thought that everything in my life that I tried to do was a complete failure. Felt like I could do nothing right. I was driving down the highway in New York, back to Staten Island where I'd live with my mom again. I'd gone from a college student and DJ to living at home with nowhere to play music. The frustration got to me and I took it out on the car's gas pedal. It was nighttime and there were barely any other cars on the road, so I kept pressing down on it, 80 miles per hour...85 miles per hour...90 miles per hour. I just wanted to get home.

As I was driving down the left lane, I approached a car in the right lane. I was going faster than it was and I'd fly by it like I'd flown by a few other cars on the road already—no big deal. But for some reason, this car decided to move over into my lane at the last second. There wasn't another car remotely close to either one of us, but this one decided it wanted to switch lanes. I jerked the wheel to the left and slammed on the brakes, and that's when it went into a complete spin. The car spun around so many times,

90 miles per hour down the highway, and then out of nowhere it straightened itself out and just kept going.

My heart was thudding in my chest. I got off at the next exit, parked, and started almost hyperventilating. *Oh my God!* My chest was tight and I could barely breathe. How the heck did that just happen? And how the heck did the car straighten itself out?

I made it home alive, back into my mother's house, and then I went back to the only place I knew I could find steady work: the cab company. Only instead of being a mechanic, I was a cab driver. I drove gypsy cabs, which basically operated the same way rideshare services operate now where you can't just flag down the car, you need to call ahead and schedule it.

The schedule was terrible, twelve-hour shifts, six nights a week (that dreaded night shift) but it was something steady. A few months into being home, I heard about a new club opening so I went and applied to be a DJ. I got the job and was able to quit the cab company since I wouldn't be able to work night shift with them anymore. Being a DJ, I'd have to make my nights available to the club. I thought I was able to escape the taxi company but as it turns out the club only survived a few months. I showed up every shift and brought the disco scene into the building, and then one day the owner came up to me and told me he was closing the place down, "Here's your last check. Have a nice life."

When that fell through, I went crawling right back to the cab company. And then again, opportunity would present itself. A passenger recognized me from the club that had closed down and told me he was in the process of opening his own. He wanted me to come along and not only be a DJ, but he wanted me to bartend and manage the place, too. Fantastic opportunities present themselves in the craziest ways. Here I was, a cab driver, and now I was going to be running an entire New York City club by myself.

Turns out, this wouldn't work so well either. There's only so long you can volunteer your time. I worked as a DJ, bartender, and manager of that club, and after weeks of not being paid consistently, I headed for the door, citing my common expression of, "Aww, heck naw."

With that opportunity now gone, I found myself on the same doorstep I'd been on so many times, head down, puppy-dog eyes looking up...

The doorstep of the cab company.

9

TURNING POINT

S ome of the expressions I've heard in my lifetime when telling my stories are, "Wow," "My goodness," "Really?" and "How is that possible? I'm so sorry that happened!" Hearing all of these expressions and seeing the reactions on faces made me start to realize just how extraordinary my life had been. All the near-death experiences in my life were more than anyone could even imagine. While they are all easy to remember—hard to forget, really—there are a few that I feel were closer calls than the others.

In July of 1976, I was visiting a friend of mine named Stephen. He lived in a house and I tried to visit him there as often as I could. No one I knew lived in a house. Everyone lived in an apartment or the projects. It would sort of make me feel good to go hang out there.

During this same time period, I was doing something a little different to make money. I started going around to bars and I'd take peoples' money playing pool. Essentially, I was a pool shark, pretending I was no good and then whooping on whoever it was that wanted to put up money to play me. I made decent money doing it but it pissed a lot of people off. So much, in fact, that some people believe the next incident happened because I took someone's money and they plotted to get it back.

One day I went to visit Stephen in his home and we were hanging out. Later that afternoon, I started walking back to my car to go back to my mother's house and had to walk through another housing project that was not mine. Some guy came up and started talking to me, asking me about money or something else, I don't really remember. Maybe it was someone I'd hustled in pool or maybe not. Whoever it was, they were only the decoy, because as they were talking to me, another guy came up from behind me with a knife and put it to my throat.

I was able to get my hand up and in between the knife's blade and my neck and it's a good thing I did. The guy who came up behind me wasn't placing the blade on my neck and telling me to hold still. He was going for the jugular. But I got my hand up and in the way, trying to fight him off while at the same time trying to fight off the guy in front of me, running through my pockets. I wiggled and wrestled and was able to keep the guy behind me from slicing my neck.

Once the guy running through my pockets was finished, he gave me a nice kick to the stomach with the sole of his shoe and then took off. That must have been the other guy's cue that they were done with me. He lowered the blade from my neck, ran right in front of me, and turned to take one last swipe at me with the blade before fleeing. It wasn't until that moment when they were both gone that I realized two of my fingers were cut almost completely off.

I looked down at my hand and saw nothing but red. I couldn't see anything else, barely even a shape. Somehow, I managed not to pass out. The sight was gruesome, but I was able to run to my car and drive myself to Saint Vincent's hospital. It was there that they wiped off the blood and saw that two of my fingers were hanging on by a thread. I was rushed back into emergency surgery to try to save those fingers and they were able to put them back on. However, I would find out during recovery that the emergency room doctor who did the procedure didn't exactly know what he was doing and while he was able to keep the fingers attached to my hand, he didn't reattach any tendons. Had my hand stayed that way, it'd be pretty much immobile with most of it.

So they had to cut me back open. I had to go back in for surgery where a surgeon would go in and reattach the tendons. All went well and I have full mobility now, but I have two pretty serious scars to forever remind me of that unfortunate walk from Stephen's house.

The story of the mugging had made it into the newspapers since no one knew who was responsible and this incident sort of reassured me that the taxi company I'd worked for so many times *was* a mafia front because I had some of the guys ask me if I wanted them to "take care of it" for me. I politely declined because I kept imagining the long and torturous ways they'd probably deal with people they "take care of" and I wanted to be no part of all that. Plus, I knew that them doing me a favor meant I'd be indebted to them. When you're indebted to the mob, you never get out. I mean, I've never been in the situation, but I've seen *The Godfather*. I know how it works. That's why when they asked me before to be a numbers-runner for them, I also declined.

After the surgery, I had a cast on my hand and was given some pain medication. I went back to my mother's house where I was still living. She was no longer living in the projects, she was able to buy a little run-down home. The place was heated with oil and when there was no money to buy oil, we would turn on the oven and open it to get some heat—this was one of those times. Money was low and I needed something different with my life. I didn't want to be a pool shark anymore, where people could exact their revenge upon me. I didn't want to drive cabs on the night shift anymore. How was I supposed to have a life and meet a girl?

I had recently applied for a new position at Willowbrook State School and I was excited about it. I last worked for Willowbrook prior to going off to college and left on good terms, so I was confident I'd get this position as a live-in counselor. The job would supply me with my own apartment and in that apartment I would be responsible for living with, and caring for, a few special needs children. I was looking forward to it—my own apartment, good job helping some kids—it was going to be great.

The day before I was scheduled to get the stitches out of my hand and get back on with my life, I got a letter from them in the mail, "We have decided not to move forward with your candidacy for this position."

How? I'd worked for them before. They knew me and knew I had experience working in the industry. How had I not gotten the job? But more importantly, I was thinking to myself, *What now?* What was I going to do with my life? Would I be a cab driver forever? Or go back to being a mechanic, coming home with dirt and grease under my nails every night? I'd already tried college and that wasn't meant to be, and I certainly couldn't afford to go back and pay on my own. What was going to become of my life? Would I live in my mother's house forever?

All these negative thoughts went swirling around in my head. That night, I was sitting around, feeling sorry for myself. It was late at night and I was out of pain pills, watching television, and then I'd lost the one thing man needs to survive.

There's a saying by Christian author, Hal Lindsey, that states, "A man can live about 40 days without food, about three days without water, about eight minutes without air, but only for one second without hope." Without hope, man cannot survive. And I'd lost all hope. In that very moment, I thought about all my failures. I thought to myself that I didn't want to live anymore. No reason to.

Then I started to think about suicide and how I would do it. I thought about going back to those projects to see if someone would kill me. Thought about all my near-death experiences and settled on the Kill Van Kull. My plan for suicide was to go back to that waterway and let it finish what it started so many years prior.

While this was going on, a new movie started on the television, *It's a Wonderful Life*. The movie is about a man who goes through troubles, contemplates suicide, and when he's about to leap from a bridge, an angel comes to him and walks him through all the positives in his life. I watched that whole movie, and once it was over and the main character wanted to live again, I broke down and cried. At that very moment in the movie, I cried harder than I ever cried. This movie saved my life. Then I went back to the thing I'd dismissed as a twelve-year-old boy: religion. I looked up at the ceiling of the house with red and watery eyes and I asked God, "Oh God, please help me."

What happened at that exact moment was something I can never explain and actually never *could* be explained. At that very moment, there was a noise so loud that it sounded like the entire world had exploded. *Boom!* The next day, people were calling into radio stations asking about it. The government tried to figure out what it was and were never able to. This is true. Crazy, but true. The very next morning, I went to the doctor's office to get my stitches removed and an older gentleman came and sat next to me. And wouldn't you know it, he started talking to me about

51

Jesus. He started talking about his church and he offered me to come and sit in, and I did. God had given me a second chance the night before and I was going to return the favor.

I went to that church the next day and spoke to a bunch of people and was presented with The Right Hand of Fellowship. The next morning, I started looking at my life differently, and there were two major things that I did that day: I quit smoking cigarettes and I quit drinking. Now granted, I was never a big drinker—I'd only been drunk once in my life, on my eighteenth birthday—but I *was* a smoker. I started smoking at twelve and didn't stop until I quit cold turkey on that very day, and I never smoked again.

Complete turnaround.

II

AFTER FAITH

10

UPHILL

Since the day I accepted God into my life again, things have progressed. They might not have progressed as quickly as I would have liked them to, but they've moved forward nonetheless.

God was always in my life, but never like He was from this moment on. I was a good Catholic as a kid. I went to Catholic school, sang in the choir, went to church every Sunday. I did it all the right way but this time was different. This time I actually *believed* in what I was doing rather than going through the motions.

Before I truly had faith, I went through the motions of someone who did: Baptism, Holy Communion, and Confirmation. But it was when I was baptized a second time that I really and truly felt like something great had happened. It was done in Brooklyn only a few weeks after that loud and unknown *boom* shuddered through the sky and I found hope for living again. From then on, I began to actually talk to God, and not in the way the church tells you to through the priest. I began to speak directly to Him and that's what made the difference (I think so, anyway).

Since I didn't have a job, denied by the Willowbrook State

School for the amazing in-home opportunity with my own apartment, I went down to the local unemployment office. It was then that I met a nice woman who was working there. "I'm going to keep my eye out for you," she told me, and she did. One week later, she called me and told me she had an amazing opportunity.

"What is it?" I asked her.

It was for a new government-funded program called Comprehensive Employment Training Act, or CETA[8]. The program was a partnership between the federal government and local government and private companies where the government would pay the first eighteen months' salary to a new employee while in training. The program gave potential employees the opportunity to prove themselves without any financial burden on the entity that hired them.

For me, the available position was a security officer within the City University of New York (CUNY) program, stationed in Brooklyn. I prayed every night for a job and when this one came, I gladly took it. I was given the job and had my uniform. I wasn't police, but I still had a badge, so that was pretty cool.

I was working as a security officer, but on the side I also began fashion modeling. Some people recommended to me that I should get into it so I gave it a shot. I was doing photo shoots and runway shows, trying to get together a nice portfolio in order to attempt to get into a modeling agency.

At the same time, I also began songwriting but the seed had been planted long before. When I was a junior in high school, I would always walk through the halls of my school singing popular songs, only with my own made-up lyrics. The lyrics were derogatory and offensive, but it was something I liked, and I'll never forget my English teacher, Mrs. Schmedes, who pulled me aside one day after hearing me and gave me an earful. "Young man, why are you singing these offensive, terrible words? It's obvious that you're talented. You're one of my best English students. Why don't you write songs that are meaningful and nice?"

Light bulb!

Her words right then ignited something I never knew I loved. I taught myself the structure of songwriting and began to create. I kept doing this, and while being a fashion model and security officer, I wrote my first song.

It was an exciting time, finishing my first song. But I was only a lyricist. I had no melody, just words formatted the way a song would be, written down on paper. And a song without a melody is only half of a song. I met a guy named Peter Roberts, who was a composer, and we finished it together. After that, I didn't know what to do. We had a song and no way to get it out there. We needed a singer so we could make a demo.

Then one day a modeling friend of mine told me about her uncle, a Broadway singer who was getting ready to sign a record deal. Then something even better happened. She said, "Hey, why don't you come meet my uncle? Maybe he'll do your demo. Who knows?"

I did meet him. We met and I showed him the lyrics and then we played some of the melody on a piano, and low and behold, he liked it. He took the song with him into a recording studio and he sang the demo for us. Now we not only had a demo, but we had a demo by a singer who was about to sign a record deal.

Finished demo or no finished demo, I got a taste of the celebrity life on New Year's Eve of 1978. The same model friend who introduced me to her uncle also told me about a party she was invited to at Studio 54. *Studio 54!?* I thought. *How in the world did you get access to Studio 54?* This was Ground Zero for disco clubs—the most famous disco club in the entire world. It was known for having A-list celebrities roaming around inside its walls, and on the night of New Year's Eve 1978, the rumors were found to be true.

"I have this famous model friend who wants me to go with her," my friend told me. And as it turns out, her famous model friend was Naomi Sims, who was coined as being the first African-American supermodel. So when my friend told me I could not only go to Studio 54 but I could go with Naomi Sims, I was in.

The night was unforgettable to say the least. My friend and I took a cab to Naomi's house and we had dinner with the supermodel and her husband. Then a limousine came, picked us up, and took us to the exclusive club. It was like living in a movie. We walked in, right past the bouncers, and there were celebrities everywhere. Drugs were all over, there were transgenders, loud music, and Grace Jones being carried out on a chariot by shirtless men. It was overwhelming.

Getting into Studio 54 was something I never could have even dreamed of, but it turned out to be too much. I felt sick, like I was in over my head or something. I'd been so lucky to get into this club and after being there for only a short while, I told my model friend that I wasn't feeling good and then I left—out the doors of Studio 54 just as easily as I walked in them—and then I was in the back of a cab and on my way home.

I never did see that girl again, my model friend, but I *did* see her uncle, a man by the name of Chuck Cissel, the one who recorded the demo for me. He liked the song so much that he told me he was going to place it on his first album. Not only did he want to put the song on his album, but he told me he was moving to Los Angeles and I was more than welcome to come out there with him. Sure!

What else was I going to do? I didn't have much going on

back in New York and moving to Los Angeles meant a chance at becoming a full-time songwriter. I accepted and was off to California, home to the stars and streets lined with palm trees. All didn't start out too well in beautiful California. Chuck's first record deal fell through but it only turned out to be a hiccup. He found a new record company under Clive Davis where he'd have a home, and once his contract was signed, he began recording.

My song wouldn't be put on Chuck's first album, but it would be put on the second. I was happy to wait. Clive Davis was grooming Chuck to be the male version of Whitney Houston, even though this was before she would become a star, and I wasn't going to complain about the wait. After all, his second album, in my mind, had the chance to be better than his first. He would have a bigger following by then. I was going to be famous. Good thing I wrote my songs under the pseudonym Gary Swann! Otherwise, the paparazzi would be coming after me in no time.

The second album came three years after moving to Los Angeles in 1982, and Chuck called me to let me know the song was going to be used. "You need to go talk to the publishers. We're going to record your song on the next album and you need to work out a contract," he said. Not only was he going to use it, but when they were in the studio and sampling the track, Dionne Warwick happened to be there and heard it, and she said it was the most original song she'd ever heard.

Really? Dionne Warwick thought that? I was doing it. My songwriting career was about to take off. The song was called "Understanding Man" and it was on Chuck Cissel's second album. My song wasn't the first single he picked but it was there nonetheless. Today, you can't just call into a radio station and ask for any old song off of an album to be played, but back then you could, and that's exactly what I did.

The first time I ever heard my song on the radio was after I made one of these calls. I was in the car by myself, happier than ever. I was screaming, "My song is on the radio! Oh my God, my song is on the radio! I did that!" I was poking a finger at the song coming out of the speaker. It was *my* song being played on the radio. One of the greatest feelings of my life.

11

UNDERSTANDING MAN

Hearing my song on the radio was surreal. When I started talking to friends and mingling with others, I told them about it and how they could hear it played if they called into the station. Everyone said they were going to do the same thing, "Yeah, man. We'll keep calling in and having the song played!"

The only problem with calling in to have the song played was that only one station in Los Angeles would play songs off of albums; KJLH, which is owned by singer Stevie Wonder. Every other station played singles and that was it. If you called and asked for something that wasn't a single, a different song off of an album, they'd say "No, we only play singles."

Chuck's first single was a success, which was good because now he could choose a second one to be released from that same album. That's how the industry would determine how many singles came off of a single album. He took mine into consideration for the second one, but in the end he chose a tune he wrote on his own. I didn't blame him for that. Why not share with the world that you can sing *and* write? His second single didn't do so well and that, in the music industry, usually means the end of that album.

So "Understanding Man" never made it as a single. The song was put on a shelf to collect dust and so was my songwriting career.

At the time, I was angry. Maybe a little embarrassed. I had told so many people about the song and its potential. I started talking about winning a Grammy and the speech I would make when I did. When nothing came of it, all those words meant nothing. Then I did what I normally did in life when something didn't work out. I went back to what I knew best. No, it wasn't driving a cab. I left that life behind when I left New York. Instead, I went back to being a security officer, this time for Pepperdine University[9].

I was a nighttime security officer at the university, and it was a Christian school, which meant there was a curfew and all the kids were in bed by 10:00 p.m. lights out. I'd make some rounds, check buildings, and by 2:00 a.m. I'd have nothing else to do. How did I occupy the rest of my shift? I went to the school's library.

As a security officer, I had the keys to the kingdom. I had keys to all the buildings so I utilized Pepperdine's library, which was one of the most extensive Christian libraries on the West Coast. The students were asleep, the lights were out, and nothing on the university campus besides me and the chirping crickets were awake. During this time, I spent hours inside that library reading anything I could get my hands on. I read the books of the early church, the Book of Enoch, Justin Martyr, and so many more. I literally got paid to study God. It was fantastic.

One night, after I'd done my rounds and was headed to the library for my normal 2:00 a.m. visit, I saw a Bible sitting on a bench outside the entrance doors. It was pretty odd that it was sitting there but I picked it up and started reading it. Admittedly, I probably should have turned it into Lost and Found, but I didn't. I kept it and it became my study Bible. I would read it every night, and it took me about six months, but I read the entire thing, cover to cover. From Genesis to the Book of Revelation.

I felt like God put that book on that bench for me. It was a sign that He wanted me to read it and become familiar with it. He knew that prior to then, I'd never read the Bible. I believed what priests and preachers would say during church services or Masses and that was it. I'd read some other Christian books but never read the actual Bible. To this day, I still have that version of the Bible in my home study. It's the Revised Standard Version (RSV) as they call it, and it was the one I had until I was made aware of a new version.

Sometime later, I went to a Christian bookstore and a worker started talking to me about a new version: The New International Version (NIV). I took his advice and I bought it, but what I did when reading it was a bit different. I read the entire thing, but I read the New Testament backwards. For some reason, it seemed like I would be able to catch something that I might have missed when I read it from front to back.

I didn't catch anything per se, but what I did realize after spending so much time studying the Bible, was that there were so many ways to interpret it. After struggling with this for a while, I decided to visit as many Christian churches as I could to understand their doctrine.

It took a year or so. During that time, I went to the churches from every major denomination you could think of. While there, I would start talking to the churchgoers who came to worship service and I'd ask them questions about things within the Bible, and for the most part, they did not seem to know what was in it. And that's not to say they're at fault. After all, how many of us have read the entire Bible? Eventually I started talking to the Pastors and Ministers of these churches. I found that many had different doctrines and interpretations. However, most seem to agree on the key issues of salvation, while some did not. I myself decided to do my best to refrain from interpreting the bible, so I took the approach of focusing on the meaning of the words and the context they were written in. Doing so, I felt, freed me from denominational influences and allowed me to be more in tune with the Spirit's leading.

It was during this time that I learned one thing that I will say to anyone I meet, and something I've always told my children: Never leave your salvation up to another human being. "Study to shew thyself approved unto God, a workman that needeth not to be ashamed, rightly dividing the word of truth." (2 Timothy 2:15 KJV)

12

LIVIN' IN LOS ANGELES

E ven though I wasn't a songwriter anymore, I was still living in Los Angeles and was still able to enjoy the perks of living there. I never had to worry about cold or snowy weather, having to rescue some little kid out of a mound of snow like my brother, Jerome, had to be after falling off of the fire escape in Brooklyn. In Los Angeles, sunshine was abundant and the temperature never wavered into "too hot" or "too cold" territory. This, I guess, was why all the film and television studios shot their movies there. They had all year round to shoot in perfect, sunny weather. No seasons to work around. Their cameras could always be rolling, and one time, I was in front of those cameras.

Sitcoms ruled the television world when I was growing up. Then as I became an adult, the trend towards reality television started to become popular. Rather than watching some scripted show, viewers were watching real people in real situations, and the infatuation spread like wildfire. It's why a majority of what we watch on television today is reality shows. Nobody wants the dryness of some show with a script anymore. They want to be on the edge of their seat, waiting to see what *unscripted* thing will happen next.

Truth is, they're all scripted, and I know this because I was on a reality show.

The show was called *Love Connection* and it began airing in 1984. The way the show worked was a contestant was shown three videos (for me, three videos of three separate women). From there, you had to choose who you wanted to go on a date with; they're made aware, you schedule the date, you pick up your date, and afterwards, you go on the show and talk about how your date went. Typical reality show, right?

Not quite.

The morning after the date, I got an early morning phone call. This was way before caller ID so I answered and heard a voice on the other end of the line ask, "So how'd your date go?"

"Who's this?"

He told me he was the producer of *Love Connection*, and then he started asking me a bunch of questions about the date, how it went, things that happened. A few days later I went into the studio for the taping of my interview and when I got there, I had this script thrown at me. "Here, read this," they said. What? Read a script? I thought I was supposed to have an interview and talk about how the date went?

Nope. With *Love Connection*, the end result is either you love the person you went on a date with or you hate them, there's no in-between, because that's what sells. So this dialogue that I had to read made me sound like I hated the girl. I was angry but I couldn't do anything about it. I was already there and I was going to read what they scripted for me, and since this was a popular television show, there were lots of viewers who saw me talk badly about this girl and how the date went. For months, or even a few years after this show aired, the reruns kept on playing. People would recognize me every now and then and they'd approach me and ask me, "How could you be so mean to that girl?" I've hated reality shows ever since. They aren't *real*. Nothing in Los Angeles is in my opinion. Except for the earthquakes.

After working a graveyard shift at Pepperdine University, I came home and went to sleep as I normally would. At about noon one day, I was woken up when the entire house started shaking. *What the...?* I had no idea. I had been through hurricanes but never an earthquake. Car alarms were going off outside, the world was rattling, and all I could think about were the rumors I'd heard so many times that California would one day experience an earthquake so great that it would separate from the continental United States and float off into the Pacific. What would I do?

That didn't happen, but this was still one of the scariest moments of my life. Not nearly as scary as my Alaska Airlines incident in 1982 though. On the way to Portland, Oregon from Los Angeles, not too far from our final approach to the airport, the entire plane started nosediving. One of the worst fears is the unknown, and when you're in an airplane that's nosediving down towards the surface, you have no idea when you'll hit. There's no window in front of you to show you how far you are from death, so as the flight was going down, my life flashed before my eyes. Truly, it did. I thought about all the close calls I'd had with death and told myself during that freefall that this was finally it. This was how I was going to die.

Somehow, the pilot of that flight managed to right the plane, but I can still hear the screams and prayers of the passengers around me as they were certain, as was I, that they were about to die.

We all lived, and had I not had so many brushes with death before, I might have been a lot more traumatized than I was. I admit, I kissed the ground when I got off that plane, and I didn't step foot on another plane for a little while after that, but I think

I would have been much more paranoid to move on with life if this was my first experience rubbing shoulders with my fate.

Los Angeles wasn't all bad, though. In 1984, the Olympics were held there, and in the Coliseum across the street from where I was working. By this point, I was no longer working for Pepperdine University. I was at the University of Southern California[10], and in order to be a security officer there, you had to go through a three-month training course similar to that of a police officer. Since we had the training and the Los Angeles Police Department (LAPD) needed extra help during the Olympics, the state granted us peace officer powers, which made me and my University of Southern California (USC) colleagues Public Safety Officers. Prior to that, USC security officers had the power to detain people until the police came to get them, but that was it. We couldn't arrest anyone. But with this Public Safety Officer title, we could.

Once the Olympics were over and I had a little taste of being a police officer, I applied to the LAPD. I had some people who worked there and they told me I was a shoo-in for a cop within the department. Listening to their advice, I applied. More importantly, I was accepted. But at the same time I was accepted into the LAPD, I was offered a promotion at USC. The promotion would make me a Sergeant and in a managerial position. Now I had a decision to make: get into the LAPD, but go back down to the bottom rung of the ladder and start all over again, or accept my promotion and turn down the opportunity of joining the prestigious Los Angeles Police Department.

I chose to remain with USC and it was a decision that changed the course of my entire life. After my promotion, I received my stripes and my Sergeant badge, and then I was assigned to the medical school. As a Sergeant, I was the supervisor. I had to make schedules and run reports. I had my own Mac computer at home and I would start bringing it into work with me. It made my job much easier being able to cut and paste and do my paperwork.

A few years later, when I was transferred back to the University Park Campus, the Chief saw me using it and asked about it. I said, "Oh, it's mine from home but I bring it in. It helps me be more organized and efficient." When he saw this, he created a new role for me: Asset Protection Manager. Making the decision to stay with USC instead of going to the LAPD had proven to be the correct choice.

13

PROMOTIONS

Asset Protection Manager. That was my new role now within the USC Public Safety blanket. I still maintained the supervisory role, but my new number one purpose was what the Chief instructed me to do, which was to oversee all the department's technology and turn the office paperless.

In my new role, I was in charge of Crime Prevention and the overall technology. I got to work right away, setting up computers as I needed them. I set up what is called a basic local area network, which was clumps of wires running in the ceiling all around the office. Being on a university campus, we were going paperless way earlier than many public companies would, but we weren't at the wireless technology stage. Not yet. But the network did its thing.

The Chief of the Department was big on education and continued learning—seemed fitting being that we were on a college campus—so he sent me to San Francisco to learn about security systems design and implementation. It was a three-day course and I absorbed a bunch of information about physical security systems and functionality (all the words that are boring to most people, but that I focused on with wide eyes). I got my certificate for passing the training and before the ink could even dry on that thing, my job had a new task for me: develop a security program for a parking garage.

The university had just bought an old warehouse that they were going to turn into a parking structure and they wanted me to design a security system that would keep it safe. The university wanted students to be able to go in and out without any fear of being accosted, having their car broken into, or any other sort of crime.

So what did I do? I reached out to G.F. Bryant, the man who had just trained me in San Francisco and was an ex-government tech guy. I told him about the project I had just been assigned and asked if he would help me design this system. He did, and once it was implemented, that parking structure was the safest one in the entire United States. Sadly Mr. Bryant passed away in 2018. He was a mentor. He will be missed.

While most parking structures have a little arm that goes up and down at the entrance, we went a little deeper than that because anybody could walk right around that and get in. We set up steel gates at entry and exit ramps to ensure no one could walk right in; we had motion sensors with 24/7 monitoring inside the structure, and we even went as far as looking into fire exits and making them double doors, spaced out so that no one who snuck into to the first could get past the second. Like I said, the safest parking structure in all the country, and it still stands and is used to this day.

It feels good to know that I was able to help students feel safe. I've always had this feeling of wanting to be nice to people and to help them and it didn't just happen while I was working at USC. While I was a public safety officer there, I also was a live-in bodyguard for actress Zsa Zsa Gabor. I would work my nights as a public safety officer, then come back to live at her Bel Air mansion and be her bodyguard. I worked basically around the clock and kept busy.

Zsa Zsa was having one of her horses shipped to Washington D.C. for Ronald Reagan's presidential inauguration. The two of them were friends from Reagan's time in Hollywood as an actor and so she went when invited. Her horse, Silver, was going to be shipped by train from Los Angeles to D.C. and I can't remember why or if I even knew why at the time, but there was an issue—the train company said they couldn't ship the horse until she paid for some specific kind of insurance. Another problem was that she was already out of town and in Washington D.C. There was no PayPal or Cash App or quick form of online payment in the early 1980s. The train company needed cash or check and that could only be paid for in-person.

Zsa Zsa was a wild lady, but one thing she was most known for with her workers was being inconsistent with payments. Basically, it was hard for the people in her life to get money from her. Due to this, everyone back in Los Angeles was hesitant to make the payment for her, but I did. I took money out of my own pocket and paid the company for the insurance so the horse could get to D.C. as she intended.

She was a hard-nosed woman prior to that and I feel like that little act of kindness softened her up a bit. She was so grateful for what I'd done to help her that she not only paid me back, but when she went to Switzerland a short time later, she bought a sweater for me and had it shipped to the house. It was a nice gesture by her but I did eventually move out of her home. It was a lot of work, being a public safety officer full-time and then coming home to be a constant bodyguard, so I moved out of there and into a nice, new apartment in Studio City, right down the street from Universal Studios. The studio would actually put some television actors up in the same building and I met a lot of them and was invited to some parties. I was even invited to one celebrity wedding. It may sound amazing—*going to a celebrity wedding!*—and it was, minus the part where some bad potato salad would cause everyone there to get food poisoning, including the bride and groom.

The work I'd done at USC for their security systems and making them paperless earned me another promotion, from Sergeant to Lieutenant. As a Lieutenant, I was introduced to a new piece of software called LenelS2 OnGuard[11], a physical security systems software. This is the system that has taken my career to the next level. God had a plan for me all along and it started with me not being picky with my prayers to Him. When I was down and out, and had no job, I never looked up to the heavens and asked for a high-paying desk job. I simply asked for a job and He gave me one, and that job led me right to LenelS2 OnGuard.

In 1999, I'd been working so well within the new security systems software that I was featured in an article for Access Control Magazine. My image was on the front cover and I had one long weekend at a conference where I felt like a celebrity. At a conference full of security systems professionals, I was approached so many times by people who recognized me from the cover of the magazine. They stopped to ask me questions, talk to me, or even to get my autograph. It was such a cool experience, one that reminded me of my songwriting days and how I was so confident that I'd be accepting a Grammy one day. I might not have been on stage accepting an award but it felt nice to be recognized for my hard work.

From that hard work, I was pretty knowledgeable in my field and my knowledge would be put to the test with USC's Y2K project. In 1999, the whole world was nervous about computers and how they would handle the switch over into the 2000s. For the entire year, every person from every industry who relied on a computer (which was starting to become almost every one of them) had this growing fear that when the clock struck midnight on January 1, 2000, all would go haywire. Sparks would fly and computers would smoke. All servers would crash and be gone forever. No one knew how these little interconnecting pieces of equipment would survive the simple change in numbers.

Our entire department stayed up through the night that New Year's Eve. Supervisors and managers who normally ended their shift before the sun went down were now sitting in the office, nervously watching as the clock ticked down to midnight. On any other year, they'd be celebrating at home with their families, but this year, the Y2K project was on the forefront of their minds. We were all ready to do damage control if anything happened, but as midnight came and went, all was quiet. No sparks. No smoke. No fire. No combusting monitors sitting on desks. The change within the system was simple and our lives went on unchanged.

Things were going well in my life and I am a true believer that this was God's plan for me all along. Although He gave me this great life, He didn't want me to forget about all of my suffering and close calls. Right around this time in my life, I was swimming in the Pacific Ocean right off of Venice Beach. I liked to go out pretty deep, dive down to the bottom, and push myself back up to the surface. I never went too deep, maybe twelve feet or so, but deep enough that the water could be well over my head.

As I was swimming, diving into the water and pushing back up to the surface, I had a moment where I thought I may never come back up. I'd gone down to the bottom and pushed off to come back up, but at that moment, something grabbed me. Something seemed to grab at my ankles and yanked me back down farther. As much as I kicked and swam, I couldn't come up above the surface. I kicked and pulled my arms through the water and I began to panic.

Then something hit me, an idea. The same type of idea that hit me as I was being pulled through the Kill Van Kull and towards the New York Harbor. The idea came to me to swim at an angle out of the current that was pulling me. So that's what I did. I swam at an angle for the surface of the water, rather than exerting all of my energy to push straight up, and I made it. My head broke the surface of the water and I took in as much air as my lungs could handle. I swam back to the beach and looked out into the water and the crashing waves, but it was like the current that was pulling me never existed, like it was hiding beneath the surface, laughing, waiting for its next victim—and if there was one thing I knew, it was that I wasn't going to be its next victim. That was the last time I ever went out swimming in the ocean, yet another near-death experience that I was able to avoid. Luckily, this would be my final one. God was giving me a great life but He wanted me to remember just how fragile this life was.

14

WIFE HUNT

When I was eighteen years old, I went through the situation with Eva and the abortion. It broke her and I can only imagine how hard that was. But I made my decision—a decision the teenaged Gary thought was the smart one. No point in bringing a child into this world if I couldn't provide them with anything. My plan wasn't to have a family or kids until I was financially and mentally ready to do so. I feared turning out just like my dad.

In 1994, my father self-deported back to Belize. I didn't have much contact with him, if any, but one day I was talking to a friend and telling her stories of my father. She told me that I had to let it all out. She said I had this hate filling up my soul and I needed to rid myself of it. So I listened. I went to Belize and visited my father, who at the time was aging and not very healthy. I talked to him and said I forgave him for everything, although he never asked for forgiveness. His response wasn't really much of one at all, but I'd done what I went there to do—I released all the resentment I had towards him.

A few years later, my dad died in his apartment and no one found him for days. He had no family or friends who cared about him and when he died no one noticed. The only reason he was found was because the other people in the complex began to smell his body as it started to decompose. I didn't want that to happen to me. I didn't want to die old and alone with no one close enough to me to care to come looking.

I was no longer a scared eighteen-year-old with no money and no path in life. At this point, I was in my early forties, I had a successful career going for me, and decided I was ready. It was time for me to find a woman, settle down, get married, and have kids. With the fear of dying alone driving me, I was determined to find a wife, but I wasn't going to find just *any* woman. I may have been determined, but I was still going to have standards. I had three requirements for the woman I would marry: 1.) She couldn't already have kids, 2.) She had to be Christian, and 3.) This would have to be her first marriage.

Being a man in his early forties and looking for a woman my age, I knew these requirements would limit me. To find a woman near my age with no kids and on her first marriage would be nearly impossible. It took me seven years to find that perfect woman and I never wavered in my requirements during that time period. I'm glad I didn't. I found the perfect woman and I intended to make her my wife. I didn't waste any time either. We met, were engaged, and got married all within the same year.

We may have gone through all the motions in a short time frame, but that didn't mean I was going to skimp out on the proposal. I knew how important the proposal was and I wanted to make sure my wife had a great one. We went on a cruise and a friend of mine from work was on the same cruise. The entire proposal was planned, so much so that even the staff members were in on it. I proposed to her on that cruise ship and then we had an Internet wedding in Las Vegas because so many people couldn't be there. Family members from all over were able to join in from the comfort of their own homes and watch. There were a few people that flew out to Vegas with us and we had a reception inside of our jacuzzi suite with them.

Having a Vegas wedding was something I was happy to do because we saved a lot of money. We were able to use that money as a down payment on a house instead of throwing it away on some huge wedding. In 2003, we bought our first place in Riverside, California and then, a year later, my wife got pregnant with our daughter. Kiana was born in 2005 and finally, after a life filled with fear of bringing a child into the world, I had my first. I knew I was ready now and the day she was born wasn't a scary one. It was a happy one. One of the happiest days of my life. I'd finally felt ready to start a family. I felt financially stable and felt good about my career, but there was one aspect of my personality that I was overlooking, and this is what hindered me from being promoted to Captain at work.

I moved around a lot as a kid, going to school in Belize, then Brooklyn, then Saint Peters, and then vocational high school. I felt like I never really stayed at one place long enough to gain a good group of friends. Every time I switched to a new school, I kept my head down and did my work but never really communicated with others. I was an introvert. In the professional world, introverts are sometimes viewed as being standoffish around others, and that, to some, is seen as rude. I never meant for it to be that way, but a lot of people at USC seemed to think that of me. For that reason, I never got promoted to Captain. I tried but they didn't seem to want to give me the distinction. So I retired from public safety work and became the USC Public Safety Department's first IT Director.

There's a passage in the Bible, that says, "No prophet is accepted in his hometown." (Luke 4:24 NIV). This is exactly how I felt. No matter how I tried to change or mend bad relationships I had, the people I worked with knew me for so long that they felt I couldn't change. I'd acted one way for so long that when I started trying to be a little more outgoing, they couldn't accept it. Eventually, I left USC altogether in late 2003.

I went to work for a security systems integration company called Henry Brothers Electronics. I took my new personality with me here. No more calling out people at staff meetings. No more blunt conversations. I planned to be much more personable—and I was.

It was while working here that I got the offer to work at NASA[12]. I'd heard through working for the company that they were starting a new security systems integration and within all of the space agency, they didn't have anyone with the knowledge or experience to work with such a system. So they put out a national search to find somebody and the V.P. of Sales from Henry Brothers came to me and said, "How would you like to work at NASA?"

"For real? Sure. I'd love to!"

"Great. But you have to move to Huntsville, Alabama."

Alabama? You mean the place in the south where they burn crosses and aren't exactly nice towards black people? You mean that Alabama?

He did.

I told him I'd have to think about it. I'd heard about all the stereotypes and even the people I spoke with sounded scared for me when I talked to them about moving to Alabama. Before I jumped to conclusions though, I did my research, and what I found was both shocking and fantastic. I found out that Huntsville, Alabama (my new home, should I have accepted the opportunity) was not only *not* a racist, cross-burning cornfield, but it was actually the second-biggest technology center in the

United States, had a low cost of living and housing, and low property taxes. Then there was one more thing that completely blew my mind, and I found this bit of information in some African-American magazine that I can't remember the name of. What it said was that Huntsville, Alabama was the best place to live and work for African-Americans in the United States of America.

Happy that I did my research, I went back to Henry Brothers and told them, "Sure! I'm interested."

15

IT ALL FELL IN LINE

I 'd heard about the opportunity at NASA and confirmed my interest after a bit of research on Huntsville, Alabama. It took a few months to hear back, but when I did, it was from a contract director at NASA. The call came in August of 2005 and what they said was that they've decided they want to contract me to come to Alabama and help them get this new security system up and running.

I thanked the man and told him, "Thank you, but I'll have to get back to you. I'm in the car with my wife right now and we're driving." What he said next to me was something I'd never heard of with any job I'd ever applied for.

"Let me talk to your wife," the man said.

"Excuse me?" I think it came more as a reflex, but I then gave the phone to my wife.

It was quiet for a bit while she listened to what he said, and then I heard my wife say back to him, "If he says he is, then he is." Then she handed the phone back to me.

The director got back on the phone and told me he needed me there in a week.

"In a week?"

I said okay and that I'd see what I could do. When I hung up, I asked my wife, "What did he ask you?"

"He said, 'Is your husband as good as he says he is?'"

One week later, I was on a plane to Alabama by myself. I stayed in some small efficiency hotel. I brought with me my finest clothes because the director had told me to dress nicely and be as presentable as possible. So I did, but my attire wasn't what caught everyone's attention.

My name is Gary McDougall. I speak properly. I'm from California and I'm fine with moving to Alabama. So when I walked into that board room on the first day to a sea of white faces, they were shocked. *Gary McDougall is a black man?* They were in awe but I guess at this point they were already in too deep. It took them eighteen months to find the right person and they never even once thought that I was a black guy.

God works in mysterious ways. I walked into that first day more prepared and charismatic than ever. I took the lessons I learned about interpersonal skills from my last job and I made sure to improve here. So after the initial shock, we were able to have a legitimate and professional meeting, talking about everything we wanted to accomplish together.

Then came the curve ball. In my very first week there, I was pulled into the director's office and told I had 90 days to prove myself or I was out. Jobless. I wanted to freak out. *Ninety days? I just moved here! I packed up my family, even my mother-in-law, and brought them here.* We'd put our California house on the market and sold it in one week. We were vested in this move and I couldn't fail.

I didn't panic, though. Instead, I worked hard to make sure I stayed. I worked twelve- and fourteen-hour days to make sure I was doing the best job I could. I came in on the weekend and worked hard to prove myself. After only six weeks, I was called back into the office and told, "You're in. No need to worry about the 90 days anymore." I've been the contracted Lead Engineer for Physical Access Control Systems since that day, administering the system for the entire space agency. On top of that, I am the first and only Black American to have held this position.

I was able to completely change my mind set with this role. I've made sure that I have an open mind when it comes to co-workers or people that I work with. I also make sure that I never make someone feel like I'm better than them. I give credit where it is due, and I go out of my way to compliment others when they do something well. My motto at work is that there is no I in team. We work together and if the team succeeds, we all succeed, and if the team fails, we all fail.

The boost in morale from that sort of work mentality was so much better for a team atmosphere. The attitude I had at previous jobs wasn't the same, but in a way I'm grateful for that. My personality drove me out of there and led me right into the arms of the NASA position that I hold and love today. My co-workers are now considered family to me and we've accomplished so many things together.

While working here and living in Alabama, I extended my family at home too, having my son, Jayden, in 2007. He had a scare a mere seventeen months after he was born. Something wasn't right with his intestines. Doctors ran tests and couldn't figure out what was wrong so they thought they might have to do surgery to figure it out. My wife and I were so distraught thinking that they were going to have to cut open our baby boy but then the Lord showed his magic again. The attending doctor had heard word through the hospital about what was happening and showed up before the surgery. She'd seen this before and had an alternative method that was noninvasive. We wept and prayed during the procedure. God answered our prayers and it worked. They didn't need to perform surgery on him after all, but they were able to fix his issue.

My wonderful family and I now live in a nice house in a nice neighborhood in Huntsville. We were initially the only black family that lived in our subdivision and it didn't seem to bother the neighbors. In fact, they kind of like my abundance of Christmas spirit.

Growing up in the projects, my dream was always to own my own home. I always envisioned having a house and being able to light it up around the holiday season. I wanted lights everywhere. That was my goal and I worked hard enough, accomplished the American Dream, and treated myself to a house full of lights. What I also have are angels that I put on display with those lights and these angels are something the neighbors like. One year I was sick and didn't get them out in time and I had someone come knocking on the door asking me if everything was okay. "Yeah, I'm just sick. I'll still be putting them up."

You know what I realized? Those angels can prevent a great fear of mine from ever coming true. If anything ever happens to me inside my home around the Christmas season and my family isn't there, the neighbors will know right away because those angels won't be up.

16

MY MOUNTAIN

I've overcome a lot in my lifetime. The fact that I am alive after everything that happened to me is surprising in its own right, but that I was able to get through so much and get to the spot I'm in today can't be some mistake. God played a vital part in it. Then again, so did my mother, which makes the events surrounding her death such a traumatic memory for me.

In January of 2009, my mother complained to my sister, Pat, about extreme pain in her knee. Mom and Pat went by ambulance to a nearby hospital where my mother was placed in an emergency room triage bed and given some pills to alleviate the pain. The nurse closed the curtain on my mother, leaving her all alone. What that nurse didn't know was that my mother had issues with swallowing pills, so my mother attempted to take those pills while in bed by herself, no call button or buzzer in the event of an emergency.

Some time later, that nurse came back to check on my mother and found that she'd choked to death. Doctors were able to resuscitate her but she was still unresponsive. Via another ambulance, she was transferred to another hospital, and on the way flatlined and brought back to life again—this time leaving her in a coma. We were told that she'd never regain her regular state of mind and, after much talk and debate with my siblings, I made the final decision to pull the plug.

On January 7, 2009, a few of my siblings stood outside the room as the doctors took our mother off life support. I stayed in the room, held her hand, and told her how much I loved her. One agonizing minute later, she was gone. The woman who saved my life twice, once when I almost choked to death on peanuts as a young boy, was now dead, the cause choking. The irony was just as sad as the reality that my mother was no longer here. That day was one of the saddest and most emotional days of my life.

I was able to move on, in time, and continue on my path of chasing the American Dream. I worked hard and I knew that God and my mother had been looking down on me, both proud. At this point in my life, I've finally reached my peak. I've worked through a lot of adversity and I was able to come out the other side a better person. God has helped me walk through this journey of mine and has shown me the ups and downs, and because of my perseverance, He has placed me in the position I am in today.

God also rewarded me with a taste of what could have been. While working at NASA, I have met and befriended an amazing singer, Kathy Yolanda Rice. Kathy and I began speaking about music while at work. We talked about a collaboration with me writing a song for her and her amazing voice bringing it to life. We did and she recorded it and then placed it on iTunes. The song, co-written by Kathy, is called, "Love Is Like A Sunny Day,"[13] and it gained some popularity and actually reached number two in the United Kingdom. It climbed the Independent charts for weeks and when the week came where it could have been number one, I remember sitting and listening to the internet radio.

In the music industry, your song really only has a certain life expectancy and if you don't hit number one by a certain point, it most likely never will. The week we had the chance to be number one came after being number two the week before. The entire countdown had played and the DJ was on the radio right before the week's number two song was about to be played. I knew that if I heard the beginning of "Love Is Like A Sunny Day" we would land at number two again and we'd have no chance of topping the chart. I held my breath for what felt like a year, waiting to see if I would celebrate or sulk, and then the DJ silenced himself and began playing the track "Love Is Like A Sunny Day". I don't think I've ever been so sad to hear a song I was so proud of. We topped out at number two and I feel like it was done for a reason. God had given me a little taste of what my life would have been if I was a songwriter. He knew it wasn't the right path for me but He also knew how badly I wanted a taste of it. So He gave it to me.

Making my work family a big part of my life is what allowed me to have the ability to work with Kathy. She still works with me today at NASA and had recently invited me to her church. It was the Westview Church of Christ in Madison, Alabama, and I wasn't going to turn down the opportunity. After all, I spent almost two years going to every church in the Los Angeles area. Why not get to know a few in Alabama?

It was Easter Sunday when I went and an interesting thing happened. The minister started talking about the incident with Peter where Jesus was arrested. As the story goes, Peter kept denying that he knew Jesus after he was arrested, and this was something Jesus predicted beforehand. In the end, after Jesus was resurrected from the dead and spoke with Peter again. Peter admitted that he did, in fact, *love* Jesus, and in this very moment during the service, I had a flashback to when I shook my fist to the sky as a twelve-year-old boy. I thought about the time where

I disowned God and all things having to do with religion. Then I thought about how close I was to suicide and how God had saved me from that moment. My story was so similar to this one that the minister was telling about Peter.

After hearing the story on that day, I decided I wanted to show my love to God one more time. I'd been baptized as an infant, then again while living in Brooklyn just days after I contemplated suicide. Now, I wanted to do it again, just to reaffirm to Him my faith and my love. So the very next Sunday, I was baptized again for the third time at Westview Church of Christ.

God has been such a huge part of my life. I've been a devout Catholic in my life and I've also sworn off all religion, but I've never been someone who hasn't believed in a higher being. I know there are some people out there who are agnostic and believe that there is nothing after death, and while I respect their opinion, I tend to ask them one thing: are you a gambler? This question throws them off, and regardless of their answer, I tell them that they must be a gambler. They're gambling on the fact that there is no God, and if they lose that bet, they could spend an eternity in Hell. For me, being wrong about believing in God means that when I die, all goes to black and that's it. I was wrong. Too bad. But I'll be dead so I'll never know any different. For an agnostic or an atheist who doesn't believe? If you die and you're right, good for you—you're right there next to me in an eternal blackness. You won't be able to brag about it or prove yourself right because we'll both be dead. But if you're wrong and there *is* a God? Well then that fiery pit of Hell is waiting for you. Is it worth it? Just to prove you're outsmarting the idea of a supreme being?

My life has been anything but a smooth ride and I believe God has been a huge part of why I was able to make it as far as I have. So I say to you, don't tell me there ain't no God, cause I know better. I have also worked hard to get where I am today and I am proof that you can overcome anything. I came from a family who had nothing and I worked my way to where I am today—I worked to attain the American Dream. If you're thinking that your life is nothing and you're down and out about what you can achieve, pick yourself up and work for what you want, being mindful that with God, all things are possible!

Epilogue

For most of my early life, I lived without faith—faith in myself, faith in humanity, faith in God. During that time, I cheated death more times than I can count. I've told these stories to people who have come and gone in my lifetime and have always received the same reaction and response, "I'm so sorry that happened to you."

Don't be sorry. There's no reason to be. Why? Because I was spared each and every time. But my question was always *why*. Why was I spared? Was there a specific purpose for me to be alive? Was there something I was destined to accomplish?

As I look back on my life while writing this book, I realize that *this* is my destiny—to write this book. To share my life's story as a testimony and deliver a message from God. To show all the bad that can happen but, more importantly, how possible it is to overcome it all through faith in God.

This book is my testimony—written in His name and for His purpose—to my children, my family, and to the world. This is my message that there is a supreme being, called God, who created Heaven and Earth. He created the first human beings in Adam and Eve, whom He loved with the greatest love ever known. To prove His love for them and their offspring, He came down to Earth as a man, Jesus of Nazareth. He allowed his creation to wrongfully convict Him, mock Him, beat Him to within an inch of his life, and then nail Him to a cross while He suffered unimaginable pain. He had the power to come down from that cross and to destroy

His enemies but He did not. *This*, I believe, is what is meant by, "For God so loved the world that He gave his one and only Son, that whoever believes in Him shall not perish, but have eternal life." (John 3:16 NIV)

After agonizing for hours, He died and was buried, but arose from the grave on the third day and was seen by many witnesses. After 40 days, He ascended to heaven in the sight of men and sat down at the right hand of His Father. At the appointed time, He will return to vanquish His enemies and keep His promise that those who believed in Him would not perish but have everlasting life.

My life has shown me that there is a God and His word is true. My life and the stories of escaping death are my proof. Therefore, I am sold out to God. "For I am convinced that neither death nor life, neither angels nor demons, neither the present nor the future, nor any powers, neither height nor depth nor anything in all creation will be able to separate me from the love of God that is in Jesus Christ our Lord." (Romans 8:38-39 NIV).

"He who testifies to these things says, Yes, I am coming soon. Amen. Come Lord Jesus. The grace of the Lord Jesus be with you all. Amen." (Revelation 22:20-21 NIV)

Notes

HURRICANE HATTIE

1   The **History of Belize** dates back thousands of years. The Maya civilization spread into the area of Belize between 1500 BC to 1200 BC and flourished until about 1000 AD. Several Maya ruin sites, including Cahal Pech, Caracol, Lamanai, Lubaantun, Altun Ha, and Xunantunich reflect the advanced civilization and much denser population of that period. The first recorded European incursions in the region were made by Spanish conquistadors and missionaries in the 16th century, who nevertheless failed to establish colonial rule. English loggers and pirates sporadically visited the region in the 17th century and the first English settlements were established around 1716. The 18th century in Belize was marked by frequent conflict between Britain and Spain and the arrival of African slaves to British plantations.

   Belize was not formally termed the "Colony of British Honduras" until 1862. It became a crown colony in 1871. Subsequently, several constitutional changes were enacted to expand representative government. Full internal self-government under a ministerial system was granted in January 1964. The official name of the territory was changed from British Honduras to Belize in June 1973, and full independence was granted on 21 September 1981

   Wikipedia contributors. "History of Belize." *Wikipedia, The Free Encyclopedia*. Wikipedia, The Free Encyclopedia, 25 May. 2019. Web. 22 Jun. 2019.

2   **Hurricane Hattie** was the strongest and deadliest tropical cyclone of the 1961 Atlantic hurricane season, reaching a peak intensity equivalent to that of a Category 5 hurricane. The ninth tropical storm and seventh hurricane and major hurricane of the season, Hattie originated from an area of low pressure that strengthened into a tropical storm over the southwestern Caribbean Sea on October 27. Moving generally northward, the storm quickly became a hurricane and later a major hurricane the following

day. Hattie then turned westward west of Jamaica and strengthened into a Category 5 hurricane, with maximum sustained winds of 160 mph (260 km/h). It weakened to Category 4 before making landfall south of Belize City on October 31. The storm turned southwestward and weakened rapidly over the mountainous terrain of Central America, dissipating on November 1.

Hattie first affected the southwestern Caribbean, where it produced hurricane-force winds and caused one death on San Andres Island. It was initially forecast to continue north and strike Cuba, prompting evacuations on the island. While turning west, Hattie dropped heavy rainfall of up to 11.5 in (290 mm) on Grand Cayman. The country of Belize, at the time known as British Honduras, sustained the worst damage from the hurricane. The former capital, Belize City, was buffeted by strong winds and flooded by a powerful storm . The territory governor estimated that 70% of the buildings in the city had been damaged, leaving more than 10,000 people homeless. The destruction was so severe that it prompted the government to relocate inland to a new city, Belmopan. Overall, Hattie caused about $60 million in losses and 307 deaths in the territory. Although damage was heavier in Hattie than a hurricane in 1931 that killed 2,000 people, the death toll from Hattie was less due to advance warnings. Elsewhere in Central America, Hattie killed 11 people in Guatemala and one in Honduras.

Wikipedia contributors. "Hurricane Hattie." *Wikipedia, The Free Encyclopedia*. Wikipedia, The Free Encyclopedia, 12 Feb. 2019. Web. 22 Jun. 2019.

THE MCDOUGALL NAME

3 **Belize Kriol** (also **Kriol** or **Belizean Creole**) is an English-based creole language closely related to Miskito Coastal Creole, Jamaican Patois, San Andrés-Providencia Creole, Bocas del Toro Creole, Colón Creole, Rio Abajo Creole and Limón Coastal Creole.

Population estimates are difficult; virtually all of the more than 70,000 Creoles in Belize speak Kriol. In the 2010 Belize Census, 25.9% claimed Creole ethnicity and 44.6% claimed to speak Kriol. Possibly as many as 85,000 Creoles have migrated to the United States and may or may not still speak the language. This puts the number at over 150,000. Kriol is the lingua franca of Belize and is the first language of some Garifunas,

Mestizos, Maya, and other ethnic groups. It is a second language for most others in the country.

When the National Kriol Council began standardizing the orthography for Kriol, it decided to promote the spelling *Kriol* only for the language but to continue to use the spelling *Creole* to refer to the people in English.

Wikipedia contributors. "Belizean Creole." *Wikipedia, The Free Encyclopedia*. Wikipedia, The Free Encyclopedia, 11 May. 2019. Web. 22 Jun. 2019.

SILVER STAR

4   The *Silver Star* was originally a service of the Seaboard Air Line Railroad, running from New York to Miami and later also St. Petersburg (beyond Tampa). It was inaugurated December 12, 1947, to replace the *Advance Silver Meteor*. The Pennsylvania Railroad carried the train between New York and Washington, D. C. under a haulage agreement, similar to the arrangement with its sister train, the *Silver Meteor*. The agreement was maintained when the Pennsy was folded into Penn Central in 1968, a year after SAL merged with the Atlantic Coast Line Railroad as the Seaboard Coast Line. Amtrak took over the train in 1971.

With the exception of a brief period from 1994 to 1995 and from 1996 to 2004, when service to Tampa was provided by the *Palmetto* (known as the *Silver Palm* from 1996 to 2002), the *Silver Star* has served both Tampa and Miami during the Amtrak era. Originally, Amtrak operated the *Silver Star* with Tampa and Miami sections that split in Jacksonville, with the Tampa section continuing on the old Atlantic Coast Line route through Orlando, and the Miami section traveling through Ocala and Wildwood over most of what was the original Seaboard route to Miami. After November 1, 2004, the *Silver Star* resumed service to Tampa, and now travels intact all of the way, backing out of Tampa and retracing its route 40 miles (64 km) east to Auburndale, where it heads south to Miami.

Wikipedia contributors. "Silver Star (Amtrak train)." *Wikipedia, The Free Encyclopedia*. Wikipedia, The Free Encyclopedia, 9 Jun. 2019. Web. 22 Jun. 2019.

I MEANT BUSINESS

5   **Staten Island** (/stætn alnd/) is one of the five boroughs of New York

City, in the U.S. state of New York. Located in the southwest portion of the city, the borough is separated from New Jersey by the Arthur Kill and the Kill Van Kull and from the rest of New York by New York Bay. With an estimated population of 479,458 in 2017, Staten Island is the least populated of the boroughs but is the third-largest in land area at 58.5 sq mi (152 km). The borough also contains the southern-most point in the state, South Point.

The borough is coextensive with **Richmond County** and until 1975 was referred to as the **Borough of Richmond**. Staten Island has sometimes been called "the forgotten borough" by inhabitants who feel neglected by the city government.

The North Shore—especially the neighborhoods of St. George, Tompkinsville, Clifton and Stapleton—is the most urban part of the island; it contains the designated St. George Historic District and the St. Paul's Avenue-Stapleton Heights Historic District, which feature large Victorian houses. The East Shore is home to the 2.5-mile (4 km) F.D.R. Boardwalk, the fourth-longest boardwalk in the world. The South Shore, site of the 17th-century Dutch and French Huguenot settlement, developed rapidly beginning in the 1960s and 1970s and is now mostly suburban in character. The West Shore is the least populated and most industrial part of the island.

Motor traffic can reach the borough from Brooklyn via the Verrazzano-Narrows Bridge and from New Jersey via the Outerbridge Crossing, Goethals Bridge and Bayonne Bridge. Staten Island has Metropolitan Transportation Authority (MTA) bus lines and an MTA rapid transit line, the Staten Island Railway, which runs from the ferry terminal at St. George to Tottenville. Staten Island is the only borough that is not connected to the New York City Subway system. The free Staten Island Ferry connects the borough across New York Harbor to Manhattan and is a tourist attraction which provides views of the Statue of Liberty, Ellis Island and Lower Manhattan.

Staten Island had the Fresh Kills Landfill, which was the world's largest landfill before closing in 2001, although it was temporarily reopened that year to receive debris from the September 11 attacks. The landfill is being redeveloped as Freshkills Park, an area devoted to restoring habitat; the park will become New York City's second largest public park when completed.

Wikipedia contributors. "Staten Island." *Wikipedia, The Free Encyclopedia.*

Wikipedia, The Free Encyclopedia, 15 Jun. 2019. Web. 22 Jun. 20

KILL VAN KULL

6   The **Kill Van Kull** is a tidal strait between Staten Island, New York and
     Bayonne, New Jersey in the United States. It is approximately 3 miles
     (4.8 km) long and 1,000 feet (305 m) wide and connects Newark Bay with
     Upper New York Bay. The Robbins Reef Light marks the eastern end of
     the Kill, Bergen Point its western end. It is spanned by the Bayonne Bridge
     and is one of the most heavily traveled waterways in the Port of New York
     and New Jersey.
        Historically, it has been one of the most important channels for the
     commerce of the region, providing a passage for marine traffic between
     Upper New York Bay and the industrial towns of northeastern New Jersey.
     During the colonial era, it played a significant role in travel between New
     York and the southern colonies, with passengers changing from ferries to
     coaches at Elizabethtown (now Elizabeth).
        Since the final third of the 20th century, it has provided the principal
     access for oceangoing container ships to Port Newark-Elizabeth Marine
     Terminal, the busiest port facility in the eastern United States, and
     Howland Hook Marine Terminal. The strait has required continued
     dredging and deepening to accommodate the passage of ever-larger ships.
     In many areas, the sandy bottom has been excavated down to rock and
     now requires blasting. In addition, the Bayonne Bridge's deck is being
     raised so that larger container ships can travel the Kill Van Kull.

Kill Van Kull translates as "channel from the pass" or "ridge". The sister
channel to the Kill Van Kull is the nearby Arthur Kill, whose name is an
Anglicization of *achter kill* meaning "back channel", referring to its location
"behind" Staten Island.
    The name "Kill Van Kull" has its roots in the early 17th century during
the Dutch colonial era, when the region was part of New Netherland.
Places were named by early explorers and settlers in reference to their
shape, topography, or other geographic qualities. The area around Newark
Bay was called Achter Kol. The bay lies behind Bergen Hill, the emerging
ridge of the Hudson Palisades which begins on Bergen Neck, the peninsula
between it and the Upper New York Bay. Behind or *achter* the ridge was
a *col* or *passage* to the interior. *Kill* comes from the Middle Dutch word
kille meaning creek. The bay was known as Cull Bay during the British

colonial era.

Wikipedia contributors. "Kill Van Kull." *Wikipedia, The Free Encyclopedia.* Wikipedia, The Free Encyclopedia, 3 Jun. 2019. Web. 22 Jun. 2019.

FALSE PROMISES

7   **Willowbrook State School** was a state-supported institution for children with intellectual disability located in the Willowbrook neighborhood on Staten Island in New York City from 1947 until 1987.

The school was designed for 4,000, but by 1965 it had a population of 6,000. At the time, it was the biggest state-run institution for people with mental disabilities in the United States. Conditions and questionable medical practices and experiments prompted Sen. Robert Kennedy to call it a "snake pit". Public outcry led to its closure in 1987, and to federal civil rights legislation protecting people with disabilities.

A portion of the grounds and some of the buildings were incorporated into the campus of the College of Staten Island, which moved to Willowbrook in the early 1990s.

Wikipedia contributors. "Willowbrook State School." *Wikipedia, The Free Encyclopedia.* Wikipedia, The Free Encyclopedia, 15 Jun. 2019. Web. 22 Jun. 2019.

UPHILL

8   The **Comprehensive Employment and Training Act (CETA**, Pub.L. 93–203) was a United States federal law enacted by the Congress, and signed into law by President Richard Nixon December 28, 1973 to train workers and provide them with jobs in the public service. The bill was introduced as S. 1559, the Job Training and Community Services Act, by Senator Gaylord Nelson (Democrat of Wisconsin) and co-sponsored by Senator Jacob Javits (Republican of New York).

CETA funds were administered in a decentralized fashion by state and local governments, on the assumption that they could best determine local needs.

The program offered work to those with low incomes and the long term unemployed as well as summer jobs to low income high school students. Full-time jobs were provided for a period of 12 to 24 months in public agencies or private not for profit organizations. The intent was to impart a marketable skill that would allow participants to move to an unsubsidized job. It was an extension of the Works Progress Administration program from the 1930s.

Inspired by the WPA's employment of artists in the service to the community in the 1930s, the San Francisco Arts Commission initiated the CETA/Neighborhood Arts Program in the 1970s, which employed painters, muralists, musicians, performing artists, poets and gardeners to work in schools, community centers, prisons and wherever their skills and services were of value to the community. The idea for CETA/Neighborhood Arts Program came from John Kreidler, then working with the Arts Commission as an intern, with the Arts Commission's Neighborhood Arts Program under the direction of Stephen Goldstine. The program was so successful in San Francisco that it became a model for similar programs, nationally. The Cultural Council Foundation Artists Project in New York City was one of the largest.

Nine years later, CETA was replaced by the Job Training Partnership Act.

Wikipedia contributors. "Comprehensive Employment and Training Act." *Wikipedia, The Free Encyclopedia*. Wikipedia, The Free Encyclopedia, 14 Oct. 2018. Web. 22 Jun. 2019.

UNDERSTANDING MAN

9   **Pepperdine University** is a private research university affiliated with the Churches of Christ and located near Malibu, California. It is the location for Seaver College, the School of Law, the Graduate School of Education and Psychology, the Graziadio Business School, and the School of Public Policy.

Courses are taught at the main campus, six graduate campuses in southern California, a center in Washington, DC, and at international campuses in Germany, England, Italy, China, Switzerland and Argentina. The Ed.D. program in Organizational leadership, (EDOL) has held international courses in China, Argentina, Chile, Belize, Costa Rica, and India.

In February 1937, against the backdrop of the Great Depression, George Pepperdine founded the university as a Christian liberal arts college in the city of Los Angeles. On September 21, 1937, 167 new students from

22 different states and two other countries entered classes on a newly built campus on 34 acres (14 ha) at West 79th Street and South Vermont Avenue in the Vermont Knolls neighborhood of South Central Los Angeles, referred to later as the Vermont Avenue campus. By April 6, 1938, George Pepperdine College was fully accredited by the Northwest Association.

Pepperdine had built a fortune founding and developing the Western Auto Supply Company, which he started with a $5 investment, but his prosperity led to his greater ambition to discover "how humanity can be helped most with the means entrusted to [his] care. [He] considered it wrong to build up a great fortune and use it selfishly." Pepperdine voiced his twofold objective for the college that bore his name, "First, we want to provide first-class, fully accredited academic training in the liberal arts ... Secondly, we are especially dedicated to a greater goal—that of building in the student a Christ-like life, a love for the church, and a passion for the souls of mankind."

By the 1960s, the young college faced serious problems. The area around the Vermont Avenue campus developed issues with crime and urban decay; tensions also arose due to the Civil Rights Movement and attempts to circumvent it such as California Proposition 14, which challenged federal fair housing laws. The situation exploded in the 1965 Watts Riots. In 1969 activists in the Watts area threatened to burn down the campus; however, they were talked out of it after all-night negotiations by then-President M. Norvel Young. In addition, the Vermont Avenue campus was running out of room to expand.

In 1967, the school began planning to move the undergraduate campus and a committee was formed to look at alternative locations, including sites in Valencia, Orange County, Ventura County and Westlake Village. Pepperdine favored the Westlake Village location until the Adamson-Rindge family, who owned hundreds of acres near Malibu, offered 138 acres (56 ha) of land. Despite concerns over building costs on the mountainous site, the school decided to move forward based on its prime location and potential for raising donations. Construction began on April 13, 1971 and the new campus opened for student enrollment in September 1972. The campus and many of its buildings were planned by Los Angeles-based architect and urban planner William Pereira.

The old campus was sold to Crenshaw Christian Center, whose minister, Frederick K.C. Price, then oversaw construction of the "FaithDome," the largest domed-church in the United States, seating over 10,000.

Pepperdine gained university status in 1971 when the school of law was added and the business and education departments became separate schools. In the 1980s, Pepperdine rose to prominence as one of the United States' leading centers of conservative politics, attracting many conservative-leaning professors from nearby UCLA and USC. Prominent conservatives on the Pepperdine faculty have included Bruce Herschensohn, Ben Stein, Kenneth Starr, Arthur Laffer, Douglas Kmiec, and Daniel Pipes.

Wikipedia contributors. "Pepperdine University." *Wikipedia, The Free Encyclopedia*. Wikipedia, The Free Encyclopedia, 30 May. 2019. Web. 22 Jun. 2019.

LIVIN' IN LOS ANGELES

10 The **University of Southern California (USC or SC)** is a private research university in Los Angeles, California. Founded in 1880, it is the oldest private research university in California. For the 2018–19 academic year, there were 20,000 students enrolled in four-year undergraduate programs. USC also has 27,500 graduate and professional students in a number of different programs, including business, law, engineering, social work, occupational therapy, pharmacy, and medicine. It is the largest private employer in the city of Los Angeles, and generates $8 billion in economic impact on Los Angeles and California.

USC was one of the earliest nodes on ARPANET and is the birthplace of the Domain Name System. Other technologies invented at USC include DNA computing, dynamic programming, image compression, VoIP, and antivirus software.

USC's alumni include a total of 11 Rhodes Scholars and 12 Marshall Scholars. As of October 2018, nine Nobel laureates, six MacArthur Fellows, and one Turing Award winner have been affiliated with the university.

USC sponsors a variety of intercollegiate sports and competes in the National Collegiate Athletic Association (NCAA) as a member of the Pac-12 Conference. Members of USC's sports teams, the Trojans, have won 107 NCAA team championships, ranking them third in the United States, and 409 NCAA individual championships, ranking them second in the United States. Trojan athletes have won 288 medals at the Olympic

Games (135 golds, 88 silvers and 65 bronzes), more than any other university in the United States. In 1969, it joined the Association of American Universities. USC has had a total of 521 football players drafted to the National Football League, the second-highest number of drafted players in the country.

PROMOTIONS

11 When Lenel was founded in 1991, competing security systems were highly proprietary and closed. Yet Lenel's founders and engineers saw the value of open architecture and streamlined integration with third-party security components.

In 1995, Lenel launched OnGuard®, the first open architecture security platform, to help customers achieve ultimate integration flexibility on every aspect of their system, from access control and video management to operating systems and databases. Today, LenelS2 provides solutions for corporations worldwide, including Fortune 100 firms, financial institutions, universities and government facilities.

With OnGuard, we continue to advance our capabilities to support our customers' current and, even more critically, their future security requirements. The open architecture that allows OnGuard to integrate seamlessly with advanced third-party technologies also enables cost-effective system migration and protection of legacy investments.

With industry-leading education, technical support, professional services and custom solutions, LenelS2 remains committed to creating a superior experience for every customer, every time. In 2018 Lenel merged with S2 Security to become LenelS2.

LenelS2 is part of UTC Climate, Controls & Security, a unit of United Technologies Corp. (NYSE:UTX).

WIFE HUNT

12 The **National Aeronautics and Space Administration (NASA, /næs/)** is an independent agency of the United States Federal Government responsible for the civilian space program, as well as aeronautics and aerospace research.

NASA was established in 1958, succeeding the National Advisory Committee for Aeronautics (NACA). The new agency was to have a distinctly civilian orientation, encouraging peaceful applications in space science. Since its establishment, most US space exploration efforts have been led by NASA, including the Apollo Moon landing missions, the Skylab space station, and later the Space Shuttle. NASA is supporting the International Space Station and is overseeing the development of the Orion Multi-Purpose Crew Vehicle, the Space Launch System and Commercial Crew vehicles. The agency is also responsible for the Launch Services Program which provides oversight of launch operations and countdown management for unmanned NASA launches.

NASA science is focused on better understanding Earth through the Earth Observing System; advancing heliophysics through the efforts of the Science Mission Directorate's Heliophysics Research Program; exploring bodies throughout the Solar System with advanced robotic spacecraft missions such as *New Horizons*; and researching astrophysics topics, such as the Big Bang, through the Great Observatories and associated programs.

Wikipedia contributors. "NASA." *Wikipedia, The Free Encyclopedia.* Wikipedia, The Free Encyclopedia, 22 Jun. 2019. Web. 22 Jun. 2019.

MY MOUNTAIN

13 Amazon Music review by Michele Wilson-Morris

Though Kathy Yolanda Rice's new single, "Love Is Like A Sunny Day" isn't a bright and sunny up tempo number as one might think based on the title (i.e., there's no bubblegum to be found here), there's certainly no disappointment on this reviewer's part. The song is about the possibilities of love, and it's a mellow and uplifting track that's musically and lyrically solid with lyrics that speak to the best feelings of being in love. But being a jazz fan, I'm looking for some sax and vocals that remind me why I'm tuning in to begin with. Kathy Yolanda Rice brings that to the table and more. This song, which is both beautiful and reflective, will definitely command any listener's full attention.

Many will play, but few will stay in my rotation list, and this cut is one that won't be revolving out. It features an above average soprano sax, and finds its home in the smooth/cool jazz category. Expectations are set pretty high for these types of tracks, and Ms. Rice does an outstanding job of meeting them on vocals, hitting all the right notes at the right time, and the band behind her is tight. "Love Is Like A Sunny Day" is filled with harmonically rich chords that provide a cozy and inviting bed of sound that complements the most refreshing new "Soulful" Jazz vocalist I've heard in some time. She could easily produce R&B hits with her voice which is warm, and layers so well with her backgrounds. Originally, Smooth Jazz came out of Jazzy R&B, like Norman Connors, George Duke, Eloise Laws, and Ronnie Laws. Kathy's music connects me with that vibe, and remarkably, this is just one single from an upcoming project. I recommend that jazz enthusiasts find this tune at CD Baby where her song is currently at the top of the chart in the Jazz/cool Jazz genre. If the rest of her work is anywhere near this good, we just might be getting a peek at the next Jazz Chanteuse in Kathy Yolanda Rice. Great song!!

Also by Gary McDougall

Published Songs

Understanding Man
Chuck Cissel
Digitally available everywhere

Love is Like a Sunny Day
Kathy Yolanda Rice
Digitally available everywhere

Made in the USA
Middletown, DE
30 October 2019